P9-DCC-641

Strategies for
Test-Taking Success:
Reading

Christy M. Newman

THOMSON
™
HEINLE

Australia • Canada • Mexico • Singapore • Spain • United Kingdom • United States

Strategies for Test-Taking Success: Reading
Christy M. Newman

Publisher: *Phyllis Dobbins*
Director of Product Development: *Anita Raducanu*
Director, ELL Training and Development: *Evelyn Nelson*
Director of Product Marketing: *Amy Mabley*
Product Marketing Manager: *Laura Needham*
Sr. Field Marketing Manager: *Robert Walters*
Associate Development Editor: *John Hicks*

Editorial Assistant: *Lindsey Musen*
Production Editor: *Chrystie Hopkins*
Manufacturing Manager: *Marcia Locke*
Development Editor: *Weston Editorial*
Design and Production Services: *Pre-Press Company, Inc.*
Cover Designer: *Studio Montage*
Printer: *Banta Book Group*

Copyright © 2006, by Thomson Heinle, a part of The Thomson Corporation. Thomson, the Star logo, and Heinle are trademarks used herein under license.

All rights reserved. No part of this work covered by the copyright hereon may be reproduced or used in any form or by any means-graphic, electronic, or mechanical, including photocopying, recording, taping, Web distribution or information storage and retrieval systems-without the written permission of the publisher except the Reproducible Answer Grid on page 168.

Printed in the United States of America.
1 2 3 4 5 6 7 8 9 10 — 09 08 07 06 05

For permission to use material from this text or product, submit a request online at http://www.thomsonrights.com

Any additional questions about permissions can be submitted by email to thomsonrights@thomson.com

ISBN: 1-4130-0924-7
1-4130-1547-6 (International Student Edition)

Library of Congress Control Number: 2005925889

For more information contact Thomson Heinle, 25 Thomson Place, Boston, Massachusetts 02210 USA, or you can visit our Internet site at elt.thomson.com

Photo Credits: p. 38 © Bettmann/CORBIS; p. 51 © Superstock; p. 116 © CORBIS; p. 146 © Index Stock.

Table of Contents

Acknowledgments

I wish to thank Phyllis Dobbins and Anita Raducanu—for all their friendship and encouragement during the creation of *Strategies for Test Taking Success*. Thanks, too, to Evelyn Nelson for her amazing ideas, and Audra Longert for her keen editing.

I'd also like to thank the following people at Thomson ELT: John Hicks, Katherine Reilly, and Chrystie Hopkins, for their professionalism, creativity, and commitment to this project.

Thanks also to Tom Friedman, my partner at Weston Editorial, with his unflagging support, energy, and vision and my children, Corey and Jonathan.

Christy M. Newman

The author and publisher would also like to thank the following reviewers:

Graciela Morales
Austin Independent
School District
Austin, TX

Mona Piñon
Oxnard Union High
School District
Oxnard, CA

Lisa Troute
School District
of Palm Beach County
Palm Beach, FL

Cally Williams
Newcomers High School
Long Island City, NY

About This Book

STRATEGIES FOR TEST-TAKING SUCCESS is a test preparation series designed to help *all* students develop effective test-taking skills and strategies. The series uses clear, easy-to-understand language and examples, with illustrations and activities. It provides support for foundation skills. It also teaches and practices advanced skills and concepts in an easy, accessible way. The series incorporates scientifically based research in the areas on reading, math, and writing.

Features

- The **instructional chapters** focus on major skills and standards concepts tested in most standardized state tests. Each chapter is divided into short lessons, called **Strategies**. Each Strategy focuses on a discrete skill or concept. The techniques rely on proven test-taking strategies.

- **Clear, simple language** and **illustrations** support higher-order thinking skills.

- The **Pretest** helps evaluate current skills. Areas-of-need are recorded on a **Skills Chart**.

- **Keys To Understanding** highlight key words, questions, and/or special test-taking pointers to learn.

- **Tips** offer practical aids and hints.

- **Practice Questions** review skills and concepts taught in the lesson. They progress from controlled to productive and open-ended questions.

- The **Review Tests** and two **Cumulative Tests** simulate the format, length, and language of authentic standardized tests. Questions ask about newly taught material and recycle what was taught earlier.

- The **Answer Key** thoroughly explains both correct and incorrect answer choices.

- The reproducible **Answer Grid** is used to practice filling in "bubble sheets" for standardized tests.

- ExamView Pro® software allows for test item customization, re-testing, and computer-delivered practice.

How to Use This Book

Students can use this book to study and review for standardized state tests. This book helps students understand what a standardized test is like. They learn the best ways to take standardized tests and practice taking them.

Teachers can use this book as a "reteach and reassess" tool to target specific standards-based skills and concepts where additional practice is needed. It can also be used for whole-class instruction or as an individual tutorial.

References

Calkins, L., Montgomery, K, Falk, B. and Santman, D. *A Teacher's Guide to Standardized Reading Tests: Knowledge is Power.* Heinemann, 1998

Chard, D.J., Simmons, D.C., and Kame'enui, E.J. "Word Recognition: Research Bases," in *What Reading Research Tells Us about Children with Diverse Learning Needs.* DC Simmons and EJ Kame'enui (eds) Mahwah, NJ: Lawrence Erlbaum Associates, 1998

Cunninham, P.M. "The multisyllabic word dilemma: helping students build meaning, spell, and read 'big' words," *Reading and Writing Quarterly,* XIV 1998

Jimenez, R.T., Garcia, G.E., and Pearson, P.D. "The reading strategies of Latino/a students who are successful readers: Opportunities and obstacles," *Reading Research Quarterly,* XXXI 1996

Reading Pretest

The Reading Pretest tells you two important things:

- **What you know.** The Reading Pretest shows you the reading skills you have now. Review those skills or start to learn and practice new ones.

- **What you need to learn.** The Reading Pretest shows you the reading skills you need to learn and practice.

Directions: The Reading Pretest has 24 questions. Twelve questions are about a newspaper article. Twelve questions are about a part of a novel.

1. Read each passage carefully.

2. Look at any pictures or extra information.

3. Answer the questions. Pick only *one* answer for each question.

4. Mark your answers on the Answer Grid.

EXAMPLE:
17. (A) (B) ● (D)

ANSWER GRID

1. (A) (B) (C) (D)	9. (A) (B) (C) (D)	17. (A) (B) (C) (D)
2. (A) (B) (C) (D)	10. (A) (B) (C) (D)	18. (A) (B) (C) (D)
3. (A) (B) (C) (D)	11. (A) (B) (C) (D)	19. (A) (B) (C) (D)
4. (A) (B) (C) (D)	12. (A) (B) (C) (D)	20. (A) (B) (C) (D)
5. (A) (B) (C) (D)	13. (A) (B) (C) (D)	21. (A) (B) (C) (D)
6. (A) (B) (C) (D)	14. (A) (B) (C) (D)	22. (A) (B) (C) (D)
7. (A) (B) (C) (D)	15. (A) (B) (C) (D)	23. (A) (B) (C) (D)
8. (A) (B) (C) (D)	16. (A) (B) (C) (D)	24. (A) (B) (C) (D)

Mark your answers on the Answer Grid.

Read the newspaper article. Then answer the questions.

Students Join Firefighters for Burned Children

1 WESTFIELD, October 20—The Community Service Team (CST) at Westfield School joined local firefighters in a special program. The program is called *Cans for Kids.* It helps the Burn Unit at Children's Hospital. *Cans for Kids* is an aluminum can recycling program run by members of the Fourth Street Fire Station and paramedics who care for burn victims.

2 "Every year, CST picks a project to help our community," says 9th grader Jamal Qualls, the group's president. "This year we picked *Cans for Kids.* Mr. Cruz, a firefighter from the Fourth Street Fire Station, came to a school assembly on fire prevention. We learned how to prevent fires, but we also learned about the victims of fires."

3 The assembly was very moving. Students cried.

They asked Cruz how they could help. He told them about *Cans for Kids.* Cruz explained that firefighters and paramedics are usually the first to arrive at fires. They witness the tragedy of burn injuries. So they have a special empathy for children who end up in the Burn Unit.

4 Three years ago, paramedics at Children's Hospital asked firefighters for help. Mia Tan, a six-year-old burn victim, needed a special bicycle to exercise her arms and legs. "We collected enough money to buy the exercise bike," says Cruz. "We learned about other expenses that families have, too. That's when we decided to start *Cans for Kids.*"

5 Westfield School now has recycling boxes next to vending machines and in the cafeteria. Each week

GO ON

volunteer drivers pick up boxes at the school. Then they transport the cans to the United Can Company's recycling center. The company pays about two cents a can. That money goes into a special account.

6   "The money pays for nonmedical items for young burn victims," says Cruz. "Our time is donated. The bank doesn't charge any fees. All the money goes to the kids."

7   Ben Fox takes care of the school building. He reports that the CST project has other positive by-products.

Not only does recycling cans help the environment, it also keeps the school cleaner. "No more cans left on windowsills or rolling under desks. I give CST two thumbs up."

8   Dr. Raisa Blau of Children's Hospital also endorses the CST project. "It's great that students are helping their peers," she says. "*Cans for Kids* is a safety net for our patients. With one phone call, my patients get what they need. Without *Cans for Kids*, I can't imagine what those children would do."

---

1   **What can the reader conclude about students on the Community Service Team (CST)?**

A   They are all freshmen.

B   They pick a new project every year.

C   They probably study environmental science.

D   They get extra credit for their work.

2   **In paragraph 3, the students cry because they are—**

A   afraid

B   hurt

C   lonely

D   moved

3   **In paragraph 3, <u>empathy</u> means—**

A   assistance

B   collection

C   clothing

D   understanding

4   **Paragraph 4 is mainly about—**

A   how *Cans for Kids* started

B   a firefighter who collects money

C   where firefighters and paramedics witness tragedies

D   why Mia Tan needed special equipment

GO ON

5 Look at the diagram of information from the passage.

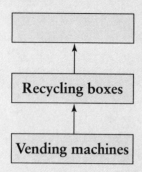

```
┌─────────────────────┐
│                     │
└─────────────────────┘
          ↑
┌─────────────────────┐
│   Recycling boxes   │
└─────────────────────┘
          ↑
┌─────────────────────┐
│  Vending machines   │
└─────────────────────┘
```

Which words belong in the empty box?

A   Children's Hospital

B   Fourth Street Fire Station

C   United Can Company

D   Westfield School

6 What does the phrase <u>positive by-products</u> mean in the following sentence?

> He reports that the CST project has other positive by-products.

A   inexpensive merchandise

B   extra purchases

C   additional good results

D   unexpected supplies

7 What word describes Ben Fox's attitude toward the CST project?

A   cautious

B   enthusiastic

C   hopeful

D   proud

8 As used in paragraph 8, the word <u>endorses</u> most nearly means—

A   praises

B   finishes

C   allows

D   votes for

9 Dr. Blau says, "*Cans for Kids* is a safety net for our patients." Using words this way is an example of—

A   metaphor

B   simile

C   personification

D   foreshadowing

GO ON ⇨

10 These are all effects of the CST project, EXCEPT—

A the school is cleaner

B Mia Tan is fine now

C more aluminum cans are recycled

D students help their peers

11 What is the purpose of this article?

A to inform

B to persuade

C to entertain

D to express an opinion

12 According to this article, what happens *last*?

A Paramedics ask firefighters to help buy a special bicycle.

B *Cans for Kids* starts.

C The Community Service Team collects cans for *Cans for Kids*.

D Mr. Cruz talks at a fire prevention assembly.

GO ON

Read the passage. Then answer Questions 13 through 24.

Adapted from *MY ÁNTONIA*
by Willa Cather

This novel is set in a remote area of Nebraska in the late 19th century. It is the story of native-born and immigrant families learning to cope with the beauty and bleakness of frontier life.

(1) I crossed the plains of Iowa on a train trip last summer when it was very hot. (2) It was my good fortune that my traveling companion was James Quayle Burden—Jim, as we call him in the West. (3) He and I are old friends. (4) We grew up together in the same Nebraska town, and we had a lot to talk about. (5) The train flashed through never-ending miles of ripe wheat. (6) It passed country towns and bright-flowered pastures and oak groves wilting in the sun. (7) We sat in the observation car, where the woodwork was hot to the touch. (8) Red dust lay over everything. (9) The dust and heat, the burning wind, reminded us of many things. (10) We talked about what it is like to spend one's childhood in little towns like these, buried in wheat and corn, under stimulating extremes of climate. (11) There are burning summers when the world lies green and billowy beneath a brilliant sky, when one is fairly stifled in vegetation, in the color and smell of strong weeds and heavy harvests. (12) There are blustery winters with little snow, when the whole country is stripped bare and gray as sheet-iron. (13) We agreed that no one who had not grown up in a little prairie town could know anything about it.

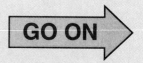

13 **What is the main idea of the passage?**

A   Strangers on a train talk about hot summers and cold winters in Iowa.

B   The towns and pastures of the Midwest remind travelers of farming.

C   A train crosses the country during a very hot summer.

D   The view from a train reminds old friends of their childhoods in Nebraska.

14 **Which of the following is the best restatement of sentence 2?**

A   I was lucky to travel with my friend Jim.

B   Jim Burden, whose real name is James Quayle Burden, was a fun-loving Westerner.

C   I met Jim Burden, also known as James Quayle Burden, who was a fortunate friend.

D   Jim Burden was fortunate to be traveling out West.

15 **Which phrase supports the idea that the train was uncomfortable?**

A   never-ending miles of ripe wheat

B   the woodwork was hot to the touch

C   oak groves wilting in the sun

D   burning summers

16 **What makes the narrator remember growing up in a little prairie town?**

A   old friendships

B   dust and heat

C   country towns and bright flowers

D   train rides

GO ON ⇨

17 In sentence 10, the narrator talks about the "stimulating extremes of climate" to show that the weather is—

A cool

B brisk

C changeable

D rainy

18 Read this phrase from the passage:

when one is fairly stifled in vegetation

What does the word <u>stifled</u> mean?

A smothered

B remembered

C filled

D forgotten

19 Sentences 11 and 12 show an example of—

A analogy

B cause and effect

C chronological order

D compare and contrast

20 The author describes nature as—

A precise and scientific

B a view of delicate scenery

C a vast landscape

D dusty and empty

GO ON

21 The first-person point of view helps the reader understand the narrator's—

A reason for traveling across Iowa

B love of farming

C thoughts and feelings

D life in a prairie town

22 The author probably wrote this passage to—

A describe the setting

B show a flashback

C resolve a problem

D use figurative language

23 In line 12, what does the word <u>blustery</u> mean?

A chilly

B freezing

C rainy

D windy

24 According to the narrator, people can only understand life on the prairie if—

A someone tells them about it

B they read a book about it

C they grow up there

D they take a trip across the country

Photocopying this page is prohibited by law.

STOP. THIS IS THE END OF THE READING PRETEST. STOP

1. ✓ Check *correct* answers. ⬭Circle *incorrect* answers.

1. B	7. B	13. D	19. D
2. D	8. A	14. A	20. C
3. D	9. A	15. B	21. C
4. A	10. B	16. B	22. A
5. C	11. A	17. C	23. D
6. C	12. C	18. A	24. C

2. Circle the incorrect answers from part 1 on the **Skills Chart**.

SKILLS CHART

Circle Incorrect Answers	Skill Area	Chapters to Study
4, 5, 10, 12, 13, 15, 19	Comprehension	Two (page 21)
1, 2, 14, 16, 17, 24	Higher-order Skills	Three (page 39)
7, 9, 11, 20, 21, 22	Literary Skills	Four (page 61)
3, 6, 8, 18, 23	Vocabulary	Five (page 87)

3. Circle the chapters you need to study. (*Hint:* You probably need to work on a skill area with two or more incorrect answers.)

Strategy 1 — Make a Long-Term Study Plan

1. **Before you study:** Think about the big picture. Think about all the steps on the way to test-taking success. Study and practice your reading skills *over time*. Don't wait until the last minute to study. Plan to make studying a *habit*.

2. **Assess your skills:** Look at the Skills Chart on page 10. Are most of your answers correct? Maybe you need to review one chapter. Then 15–20 minutes a day may be enough study time. Or you may need to study more chapters. Then an hour or more a day may be enough time.

Photocopying this page is prohibited by law.

3. **Make your plan:** Count your study days between today and the test. Don't count the days when you are very busy.

Sun	Mon	Tue	Wed	Thu	Fri	Sat
	1 *Today:* *Make a* *plan*	2 *5:00–6* *Study* *time*	3 *5:00–6* *Study* *time*	4 *5:00–6* *Study* *time*	5 *5:00–6* *Study* *time*	6 *5:00–6* *Study* *time*
7	8 *5:00–6* *Study* *time*	9 *5:00–6* *Study* *time*	10 *Study for* *science* *test*	11 *5:00–6* *Study* *time*	12 *5:00–6* *Study* *time*	13 *5:00–6* *Study* *time*
14	15 *5:00–6* *Study* *time*	16 *5:00–6* *Study* *time*	17 *5:00–6* *Study* *time*	18 *5:00–6* *Study* *time*	19 *Birthday* *party* *for Dad*	20 *5:00–6* *Study* *time*
21	22 *5:00–6* *Study* *time*	23 *5:00–6* *Study* *time*	24 *5:00–6* *Study* *time*	25 *5:00–6* *Study* *time*	26 *5:00–6* *Study* *time*	27 *School* *play*
28	29 *5:00–6* *Study* *time*	30 *5:00–6* *Study* *time*	31 TEST			

4. **Decide how long to study each day:** Write the time you need to study on a calendar or in a notebook. Check off each day when you finish your work.

5. **Strategize for success:** Keep to your plan. That way you will be prepared. You won't get stressed out. You won't have to cram (study just before the test). Instead, you can relax and get a good night's sleep. You will be ready on the day of the test.

It is helpful to know what is on the reading test. This section tells about three kinds of questions. It also gives you strategies for answering questions.

Types of Test Questions

1. **Multiple Choice:** Every test has many multiple-choice questions. (All questions on the Reading Pretest are multiple choice.)

   A multiple-choice question has two parts: a **stem** and **answer choices**. The stem is the **question**. There are usually four answer choices. You pick **one**.

The author wrote this passage to—

   A. describe the setting

   B. show a flashback

   C. resolve a problem

   D. use figurative language

The **stem** is *the question.*

The **answer choices** are *A, B, C,* or *D.*

Photocopying this page is prohibited by law.

2. **Short Answer:** Some standardized tests also have **short-answer** questions. For these, you write the answer. Short answers are one or two sentences. Sometimes icons (small pictures) let you know that a question is a short-answer question.

 What are paragraphs 3 and 4 mainly about?

 Why did the family give money to Ms. Alvarez?

Short-answer questions take about five minutes to read, think about, and answer. You will have lines like these to write on:

_____

_____

_____

3. **Open Response:** Open responses are also called **extended responses** or **writing tasks**. You write an answer to these questions, too. But these answers are longer than one or two sentences. Open-response questions take 10 to 15 minutes to answer.

 Why did Rigoberta Menchú win the Nobel Peace Prize? Support your answers with details and information from the article.

Most questions on state tests are **multiple-choice questions**. You pick the best answer from four choices. This lesson shows you how to get the right answer.

1. **Read the passage carefully.**

   - Underline or circle important words or facts.

   - Underline or circle new or difficult words.

   - Take notes.

	My Notes
(1) Most people don't know how potato chips were invented. (2) The first potato chip was fried in 1853. (3) At dinner one night, Cornelius Vanderbilt, the railroad millionaire, complained to his chef. (4) "These fried potatoes are too thick," he said. (5) The chef was furious. (6) To retaliate, the angry cook cut the potatoes as thin as paper. (7) He fried them in oil. (8) He put a lot of salt on them. (9) Then he served them. (10) But the chef got a big surprise. (11) Vanderbilt and his guests loved these new potato "chips." (12) That's how this popular snack food started.	invention date fact means the same cooking details

Photocopying this page is prohibited by law.

2. **Read the questions carefully.**

- Look for important question words or phrases (*when, who, why, how much*).

- Use line or paragraph numbers. Many readings have numbers to help you find information quickly ("According to *sentence 3...*" or "In *paragraph 6...*").

Read the sentence. Use the sentence number to find the answer.

EXAMPLE

In sentences 3 and 4, you learn that Cornelius Vanderbilt doesn't like—

____ A. fried potatoes   ✓ B. thick potatoes

According to sentence 10, the chef was—

   ____ A. furious   ____ B. surprised

The chef was furious in sentence 5. But the question asks about sentence 10. So the answer is B. Sentence 10 says: *But the chef got a big surprise.*

3. **Pick one answer.** These steps can help you pick the right answer.

Step 1 Read the *stem*. Think of an answer in your own words.

Step 2 Find the answer choice that is most like your answer.

Step 3 Mark only *one* answer. Sometimes two choices seem right. Consider the differences between them. Read the stem again. Pick the *best* answer.

4. **Answer every question.** Don't leave any blanks on the answer sheet. Some questions are hard. You may not know an answer. Then it's time to **guess**. Use the **process of elimination** to make your best guess.

EXAMPLE

Martha wants to answer Question 2.

2. What is the most important idea in the paragraph?
   A. A chef made the first potato chip in 1953.
   B. Potato chips were invented by accident.
   C. Potatoes are healthy and high in vitamin C.
   D. Vanderbilt was pleased with the potato "chips."

First, Martha reads the stem: *What is the most important idea in the paragraph?*
She thinks: *The **most important idea** has to be about the whole passage. It is general.* But she doesn't know the answer yet.

Next, she looks at the four choices. She still doesn't know the answer.

Then, she uses the **process of elimination** to make her best guess. The process of elimination helps her cross out wrong answers.

Photocopying this page is prohibited by law.

Step 1 Cross out answers you know are wrong.

The first potato chip was made in **1853**. Martha knows A is wrong.	A̶. A chef made the first potato chip in 1953.

Step 2 Use information only from the passage. Cross out answers about anything NOT in the passage.

Martha sees no information about *healthy* or *vitamin C*. She crosses out C, too.	C̶. Potatoes are healthy and high in vitamin C.

Step 3 Make sure an answer is true.

Martha rereads part of the paragraph. B and D are both true. Martha can't cross them out.	B. Potato chips were invented by accident. D. Vanderbilt was pleased with the potato "chips."

Step 4 Read the stem again. Then make your best guess.

Martha reads the stem again. She thinks: *I'm looking for the* most important idea, *not a* detail. *This paragraph is the story of how potato chips were invented. Vanderbilt liked the potato chips. But that's only in one sentence. I think that's a* detail, *not the* most important idea.

Martha makes her best guess. She marks B on the answer sheet. Do you agree?

Martha is correct. B is the best answer.

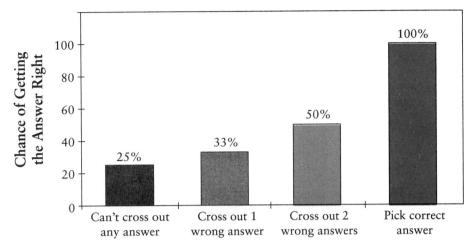

The Process of Elimination: How Guessing Helps Your Score

1 question with 4 answer choices

Here's how the **process of elimination** works:

1. You can't cross out ANY answers. The chance of a right guess: 25%.

2. You CAN cross out **1** wrong answer. The chance of a right guess: 33%.

3. You can cross out **2** wrong answers. The chance of a right guess: 50%!

4. You can cross out **3** wrong answers. You score! That's 100%!

Use these successful strategies as you work in this book and take tests.

1. Read all directions carefully. Don't skim. Ask the test giver questions about the directions.

2. Pay attention to paragraph numbers ("In *paragraph 8,* the author. . .") or line numbers ("According to *lines 17–18,* what does. . .") in the stem. These numbers tell you where the answer is.

3. Answer easy questions first.

4. Don't spend a lot of time on one question. If you're stuck, skip it. You can look at it again after you answer the easy questions. Make sure you have enough time for all questions.

5. Don't change your answer unless you are sure your first answer is wrong.

6. Fill in the answer sheet carefully. Make sure you put your answer in the right place.

Build Comprehension Skills

Understand Main Idea and Supporting Details

Main Idea

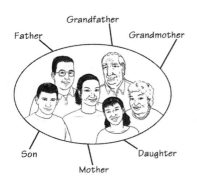

Grandfather

Father

Grandmother

Son

Mother

Daughter

The **main idea** is the most important idea in a reading. It is a *general statement*. When someone asks *What is this about?* the answer is the main idea.

> **EXAMPLES**
>
> A. It's about a boy lost in the wilderness.
>
> B. It's a biography of Martin Luther King, Jr.
>
> C. It tells you how to pick a good password.

The main idea is often in the *first sentence* in a passage.

> **TIP**
>
> **Titles** can help you find the main idea:
>
> *The Louisiana Purchase*
>
> *How to Install Your New Software*

> **EXAMPLES**
>
> A. She rode a horse named Fina when women didn't ride.[1]
>
> B. The scientific method is a way to look at data.
>
> C. Thousands of people visit Seward, Alaska, for the Polar Bear Jump Off, but only 50 people jump in the water.

[1] From Jennifer Trujillo, "The Race" in *Love to Mamá: A Tribute to Mothers* (New York: Lee and Low Books, Inc., 2001).

The main idea can be in the *last sentence*, too.

EXAMPLES

A. That's why I am voting for the tax increase.

B. She had been nice enough to pay me double for cleaning out her attic, and I had stolen her fortune.[2]

C. So you can see, it's important to take care of nature.

Underline the main idea of this paragraph.

Vietnam's Math Prizes for Girls

The Sadosky prizes are important math prizes for girls in Vietnam. They are named for Cora Sadosky. She was a mathematician from Argentina. Each year four girls win Sadosky prizes. Those girls have the best math scores in all of Vietnam. Winners get awards and money. They also travel to math contests in countries such as Greece, Japan, and the United Kingdom. Nowadays, more girls study math because Sadosky winners are famous in Vietnam.

Answer: You are correct if you underlined the first sentence. The first sentence is the main idea of the paragraph. It tells what the paragraph is about.

 Keys to Understanding

Signal Questions: Main Idea
What is the *best title* for the reading passage?
What is the *topic sentence* in paragraph 1?
Which of the following best states the *main point* of the poem?

Check the question that asks about a main idea.

—— A. What does *mathematician* mean?

—— B. What is this paragraph mainly about?

B is correct. The signal is *mainly about*. A asks for a definition. It is a vocabulary question.

[2] From Dan Gutman, *Honus and Me* (New York: Avon Books, 1997).

Our Family

Supporting details help you understand the main idea. They are specific, not general.

TIP

Look at the paragraph about the Sadosky prizes on page 24 again. The sentences after the main idea are **supporting details**.

SUPPORTING DETAILS

Type	Example
fact	There are 12 months in a year.
	Cora Sadosky was a mathematician.
example	Yes, I like vegetables. For instance, I had carrots at lunch.
	Winners also travel to competitions in countries such as Greece, Japan, and the United Kingdom.
explanation	He goes to the library after school because his parents work.
	Nowadays, more girls study math because Sadosky winners are famous in Vietnam.

Keys to Understanding

Signal Questions: Supporting Details

wh-questions: *Who, What, Where, When, How much,* or *How many*

Example: *Who* is Cora Sadosky? *Where* is she from? *How much* is the prize?

Check the question that asks about a supporting detail.

—— A. How many girls win Sadosky prizes each year?

—— B. What is the topic sentence of this paragraph?

A is correct. *How many* signals specific information. B is incorrect. A *topic sentence* signals the main idea.

Practice: Read the paragraph and answer the questions.

Seeing Triple

1   Maria is short. Her hair is long and straight. Aldo is medium height and curly haired. Otto is very tall with dark blond hair. People are often surprised to hear that they are related. But when it turns out that they are triplets, people are *really* surprised.

2   That's why the Gomez triplets love to go to the Triplets Convention in California. The convention is the only place in the world where triplets feel ordinary. This year there are over 100 sets of triplets, from children to adults. Maria, Aldo, and Otto from Mexico meet Lisa, Anne, and Tom from the United States. They live in different countries. But they have a lot in common.

3   "Do people ask if you always dress the same, even when you are wearing different clothes?" Lisa asks. The friends all nod and laugh.

4   "And they're always surprised that I don't look like Aldo and Otto!" says Maria, giggling.

5   "People even ask if we're the same age!" jokes Tom. "Sometimes I want to say no, but I never do."

1. What is the main idea in paragraph 1? Check the correct answer.

    —— A. The Gomez triplets don't look alike.

    —— B. The Gomez triplets are from Mexico City.

    —— C. Otto is the tallest triplet.

2. Write *fact, example,* or *explanation* next to the sentences.

    Example: Otto is very tall with dark blond hair. ——*fact*——

    A. That's why the Gomez triplets love to go to the Triplets Convention in California. ——————————

    B. This year there are over 100 sets of triplets, from children to adults. ——————————

    C. "Do people ask if you always dress the same, even when you are wearing different clothes?" ——————————

SEE PAGE 169 FOR ANSWERS.

Recognize Sequence and Chronology

Actions happen in **order**, or **sequence**.

First

Next

Last

Chronological order is time order.
2005, 2006, 2007, 2008, 2009, 2010

Alphabetical order is letter order.
a b c d e f g h i j k l m n o p q r s t u v w x y z

Numerical order is number order.
1, 2, 3, 4, 5, 6, 7, 8, 9, 10

Write the kind of order.

EXAMPLE
Step 1: Beat 2 eggs in a bowl
Step 2: Add 3 cups of flour
Step 3: Add 1 T of baking soda

___numerical___

TO DO
10 am: meet Mr. Chang
12 pm: lunch at Greystone
3 pm: dentist appt.
7:30 pm: movie w/Carmen

A. _____

Alma
Faisal
Javier
Mari
Tanh

B. _____

A is a schedule. It shows *chronological* order. B is in *alphabetical* order. It is a class list.

Keys to Understanding

Signal Words: Sequence and Chronology

First	Middle	Last
At first	Second/Third/Fourth . . .	At last
In the beginning	Then/Next	Finally
At the start	After/After that	In the end
	Later/Following that	

Check the sentence that shows sequence.

_____ A. Aliya is seven years old.

_____ B. Aliya is the seventh girl in line.

Answer B is correct. It describes a line of students. Aliya is the seventh in a sequence of students. Answer A has the word *seven,* but it is an age. It is not part of a sequence.

A day or date, a month or season, and a time are also signal words.

Day or **Date**	**Month** or **Season**	**Time**
On Thursday	In September	At noon
On July 4, 1776	In the fall	At 5:15

Check the sentences that show sequence.

_____ A. I play tennis in the spring. Then, in summer, I swim every day.

_____ B. My birthday is on August 5th. I'm on vacation then.

Answer A is correct. The words *in the spring* and *Then, in summer,* show a chronology, or time order. In B, August 5th is a single date, not a sequence.

Practice A: Complete the sentence. Then write labels on the drawers.

Put the labels in _____ order.

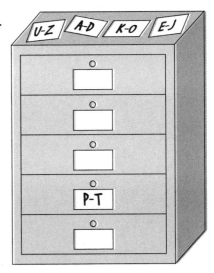

Practice B: Underline the sequence or chronology words in the sentences. Then complete Ana's schedule.

✔ Ana Garcia has art ___at 12:30___.

1. Latin is her last class.

2. Science is Ana's first class of the day.

3. Next, she has English with Mr. Hooley.

4. At noon she meets her friends for lunch.

5. Before lunch she plays the flute in band.

6. She has history in the afternoon.

7. She has math _____.

Name:	_Ana Garcia_
8:00	———————
9:00	———————
10:00	———————
11:00	———————
12:00	———————
12:30	_art_
1:30	———————
2:30	———————

SEE PAGE 169 FOR ANSWERS.

Compare and Contrast

Good readers **compare** and **contrast** as they read.

To **compare:** Find what is *alike (similar)* or the *same.*
To **contrast:** Find what is *different (dissimilar).*

Sarah and Pablo bring lunch to school. Compare and contrast their lunches. How are their lunches alike? How are their lunches different?

Look at the Compare and Contrast Chart. Three foods are missing. Write the missing foods in the chart.

	Sarah	**Pablo**
Compare	sandwich fruit _____	sandwich fruit _____
Contrast	cheese cookies _____	tuna carrots _____

To compare, Sarah and Pablo both have milk. To contrast, Sarah has an apple. Pablo has a banana.

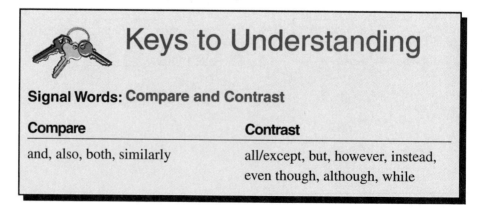

Keys to Understanding

Signal Words: Compare and Contrast

Compare	**Contrast**
and, also, both, similarly	all/except, but, however, instead, even though, although, while

Check the sentence that shows contrast.

_____ A. All my friends eat lunch at school, except Somsy.

_____ B. Sarah eats lunch at school, and Pablo eats with her.

Sarah and Pablo eat in the *same* place. Somsy eats in a *different* place. That is a *contrast*. The words *All/except* show contrast, too. So A is correct. B compares.

Practice A: Read the sentences. Underline the signal words. Write *CP* next to sentences that compare. Write *CT* next to sentences that contrast.

EXAMPLE

__*CT*__ Sarah always drinks milk. Pablo has juice <u>instead</u>.

_____ 1. Pablo brings his lunch from home. Sarah does also.

_____ 2. Pablo doesn't like sweets. Sarah, however, loves sweets.

Practice B: Compare and contrast Jean-Paul and Marc. Write four sentences. Use information from the chart. Use signal words. Write on your own paper.

EXAMPLE

Jean-Paul is from the United States; however, Marc is from Haiti.

	Jean-Paul	**Marc**
Compare	Last name: Rue Address: 2 Bay St. City: Midland	Last name: Rue Address: 2 Bay St. City: Midland
Contrast	Age: 14 Mother: Angeline Rue Born in: United States	Age: 36 Wife: Angeline Rue Born in: Haiti

SEE PAGE 169 FOR ANSWERS.

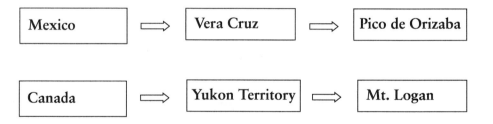

Strategy 6

Use Graphic Aids

Graphic aids show information, or data. Tables, flowcharts, graphs, and maps are graphic aids. They help you compare and contrast information, too.

These graphic aids have information about the tallest mountains in North America.

1. **Table:** Information in rows (across) and columns (down)

TALLEST MOUNTAINS IN NORTH AMERICA

Rank	Mountain	Country
1.	Mt. McKinley	United States
2.	Mt. Logan	Canada
3.	Pico de Orizaba	Mexico

2. **Flowchart** or **Sequence Web:** Information in groups or categories

Tallest Mountains in North America

Mexico	⟹	Vera Cruz	⟹	Pico de Orizaba

Canada	⟹	Yukon Territory	⟹	Mt. Logan

Complete the flowchart. Use information from the table about the tallest mountains.

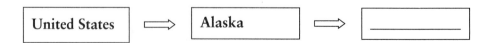

United States	⟹	Alaska	⟹	_____

The order of this flowchart is: country, state/territory, mountain. The last box is a mountain, *Mt. McKinley*.

3. **Graphs:** Information with bars, lines, or circles. This graph has a legend, or key. Legends show extra information about a graph.

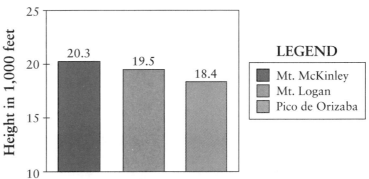

Tallest Mountains in North America

4. **Maps:** Information about places and geography. Maps can have legends, too.

Check the true statement.

____ A. There is only one kind of useful graphic aid.

____ B. There are many kinds of useful graphic aids.

Many kinds of graphic aids help show information. Answer B is correct.

Practice A: Complete the sentences. Use the graphic aids on pages 30 and 31. Write the graphic aids you use.

Sentence	Graphic Aids
Example: The tallest mountain in Canada is <u>Mt. Logan</u>.	table, flowchart

1. The tallest mountain in North America is _____.

2. It is in the state of _____.

3. Pico de Orizaba is in the state of _____.

4. Mt. McKinley and Mt. Logan are near the _____ Ocean.

5. Mt. _____ is about 1,000 feet taller than Pico de Orizaba.

Practice B: Complete the sentences. Use the words below.

Compare	Contrast
both, similarly	but, however, instead

EXAMPLE

Logan and McKinley are English names; de Orizaba, <u>however</u>, is Spanish.

---

1. Mt. McKinley and Mt. Logan are _____ north of Mexico.

2. Mt. Logan is near an ocean. Pico de Orizaba is near a gulf _____.

3. Pico de Orizaba has snow on top. Mt. McKinley and Mt. Logan are _____ snow topped.

4. The mountains are all over 15,000 feet high, _____ only Mt. McKinley is over 20,000 feet.

SEE PAGE 169 FOR ANSWERS.

CHAPTER 2: REVIEW TEST

Review the steps in the process of elimination and test-taking strategies on pages 13–20. Then use these strategies to take the Chapter Review Test. Mark your answers on the Answer Grid.

> **Read the brochure and look at the map. Then read the biography note. The brochure is about the National Mall in Washington, D.C. The biography note is about Maya Lin. Answer Questions 1 through 9.**

Come Visit the National Mall

1   The National Mall in Washington, D.C., is a treasury of our national heritage. The Mall is a long, rectangular park. It runs from the Lincoln Memorial to the Capitol Building. The Washington Monument is on the Mall. So is the Vietnam Veterans Memorial. The Mall is bordered by wonderful museums. Everything is within walking distance, so wear comfortable shoes. The National Park Service offers bus rides with tour guides, too.

2   The Mall is known for its beauty, history, and culture. But it's also a place to think, to remember, and to protest. Dr. Martin Luther King, Jr.'s "I Have a Dream" speech, for example, was delivered on the steps of the Lincoln Memorial.

3   Our tour begins at the (1) Lincoln Memorial. There's a statue of Lincoln

The National Mall

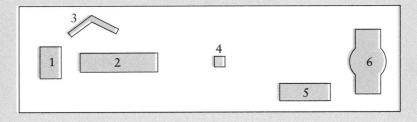

(Continued on next page)

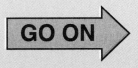

sitting in a chair. His expression is very serious as he looks out over the (2) Reflecting Pool. The Gettysburg Address and Lincoln's second inaugural address are carved on the walls inside.

4   Nearby is the (3) Vietnam Veterans Memorial. It's a black granite wall engraved with the names of those who died while serving in the war. Visitors and veterans search the wall for the names of family members and friends. They leave pictures and flowers—and tears—at this memorial.

5   Next is the (4) Washington Monument. It is 500 feet tall. It towers over everything. The elevator to the top takes 70 seconds—or you can walk up 897 steps.

6   It's a short walk to the (5) Smithsonian Air and Space Museum. Nearly 10 million people visit it each year. Look up when you get inside. The Wright Brothers' 1903 *Flyer*, Lindbergh's *Spirit of St. Louis*, and the *Apollo 11* lunar module are hanging from the ceiling.

7   Our last stop is the (6) Capitol Building. The entrance is the Rotunda. It is a huge, circular room, 96 feet around and 180 feet high. The House of Representatives meets in the south wing of the Capitol. The Senate meets in the north wing. You can even visit the members of Congress who represent you!

8   Now it's time to soak your feet, relax, eat dinner, and plan your next visit.

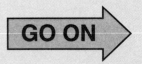

Biography Note: Maya Lin

Lin, Maya (1959–) Born: Athens, Ohio; architect, sculptor.

Maya Lin is best known for the Vietnam Veterans Memorial in Washington, D.C. Lin's family came to the United States from China in 1948. She studied architecture at Yale University. Lin entered a contest during her senior year. She designed a memorial to honor the Vietnam War veterans. Her plan won out over 1,420 others. It was a simple V-shaped wall of shiny black granite. The names of more than 58,000 Vietnam casualties are on it. Lin said, "The cost of war is these individuals. And we have to remember them first." Lin's wall is different from other war memorials. They can be made of granite, too. But they often show heroes in battle. Some people didn't like Lin's design. They called it "a black scar." They were also angry because Lin is an Asian American. The Vietnam War was in Asia. But Lin fought back. She believed in her plan, and she was right. Millions of people visit the monument every year. They stand in front of it and cry. Lin has designed other memorials and buildings. She has won many awards. A movie about her won an Academy Award in 1995.

GO ON

Use the brochure to answer Questions 1 through 5.

1 Paragraphs 1 and 2 are mainly about—

  A Dr. King's speech

  B Washington's best shopping mall

  C what to visit on the National Mall

  D how to get to the top of the Washington Monument

2 The numbers on the map probably—

  A show the places described in the brochure

  B are directions to the Mall

  C show the correct order to see places on the Mall

  D help the National Park Service plan good bus routes

---

3 Look at the flowchart.

What belongs in the empty box?

  A National Park Service

  B White House

  C Washington Monument

  D Smithsonian Air and Space Museum

4 What three places are closest to each other?

   A the Lincoln Memorial, the Reflecting Pool, the Capitol

   B the Vietnam Veterans Memorial, the Washington Monument, the Reflecting Pool

   C the Capitol, the Smithsonian Air and Space Museum, the Vietnam Veterans Memorial

   D the Smithsonian Air and Space Museum, the Vietnam Veterans Memorial, the Lincoln Memorial

5 What information is not in the brochure?

   A The National Mall is a rectangular park.

   B The Gettysburg Address is on the Lincoln Memorial.

   C *Apollo 11* landed on the moon on July 20, 1969.

   D The Senate meets in the north wing of the Capitol.

Use the biography note for Question 6.

6 How is the Vietnam Veterans Memorial different from traditional monuments?

   A Traditional monuments can be made of granite.

   B A woman designed the Vietnam Veterans Memorial.

   C Traditional monuments often show heroes in battle.

   D It is a black scar.

Use the brochure *and* the biography note to answer Questions 7 through 9.

7 What happens last?

   A People search the wall for names.

   B Maya Lin fights for her design.

   C Maya Lin studies architecture.

   D Some people oppose Maya Lin's design.

8 All these sentences show that the Vietnam Veterans Memorial brings out strong feelings, EXCEPT

   A They leave pictures and flowers—and tears—at this memorial.

   B Her plan won out over 1,420 others.

   C They called it "a black scar."

   D Lin said, "The cost of war is these individuals."

9 What information is in both the brochure and the biography note?

   A The Vietnam Veterans Memorial is black.

   B The Washington Monument is 500 feet tall.

   C Maya Lin is an architect.

   D The Capitol Rotunda is round.

GO ON

Photocopying this page is prohibited by law.

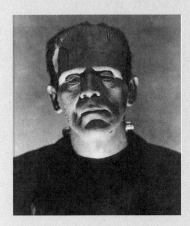

Frankenstein by Mary Shelley is a very famous horror story. There are over 250 editions today. The novel is translated into many languages. Directors love making movies of *Frankenstein*. Most are scary, like horror movies today. But some *Frankenstein* movies are sad, and some are even funny. Many experts call *Frankenstein* the world's first science fiction novel. Before *Frankenstein*, there was no use of science in horror stories. But Dr. Frankenstein was a man of science. He was a doctor. He used electricity with his monster.

The story of Frankenstein is almost 200 years old. Yet today there are websites about him just like there are websites about Freddie Kruger and Chuckie. *Frankenstein* was written by a teenager. Mary Shelley was only 19 years old when she wrote it. And Frankenstein is the *scientist*, not the monster. So you see, *Frankenstein* is still surprising us today!

10 A good title for this passage is—

   A The World's First Science Fiction Novel

   B Strange Monsters on the Internet

   C Mary Shelley, Teenage Horror Writer

   D Facts about *Frankenstein*

11 How is *Frankenstein* different from the horror stories before it?

   A The monster is very big.

   B It's funny.

   C It is science fiction.

   D It is on a website today, not in a book.

12 How are *Frankenstein* movies like other horror movies today?

   A They are scary.

   B They are sad or funny.

   C Teenagers write them.

   D They are scientific.

13 What came first?

   A horror movies

   B scary stories

   C science fiction

   D translations of *Frankenstein*

STOP. THIS IS THE END OF THE REVIEW TEST.
SEE PAGE 169 FOR ANSWERS AND EXPLANATIONS.

Strategies for Test Taking Success: Reading © Thomson Heinle

Strategy 7   Understand Cause and Effect

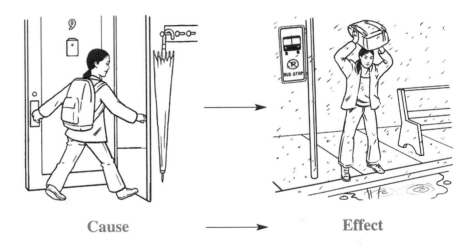

Monday, 7:00 A.M.   Monday, 7:30 A.M.

Cause ⟶ Effect

> **TIP**
>
> The cause always happens first. The effect happens after the cause.

A **cause** *makes* something happen. An **effect** is *what* happens.

Check the sentence that shows cause.

____ A. Marissa gets wet.

____ B. Marissa leaves her umbrella at home.

The answer is B. Marissa gets wet (the effect) *because* she left her umbrella at home (the cause). First, she leaves her umbrella at home. Second, she gets wet.

Check the sentence that shows effect.

____ A. Chan sees that it's raining.

____ B. Chan takes his umbrella and stays dry.

The answer is B. First, Chan sees the rain (the cause). Second, he takes his umbrella and stays dry (the effect).

Keys to Understanding

Signal Words: Cause and Effect

Cause	Examples
as a result of, because, for, since	Slavery ended in the United States *because* the Union won the Civil War. *Since* there was no oxygen in the jar, the flame went out.

Effect	Examples
brought about, consequently, led to, which is why, so, therefore	The Union won the Civil War, which *brought about* the end of slavery in the United States. There was no oxygen in the jar *so* the flame went out.

Signal Questions: Cause and Effect

To find a cause, ask:	To find an effect, ask:
Why did that happen?	What happened after that?
What made that happen?	What was the result of that?
How did that happen?	What did that do?
What factor contributed to that?	
What caused that?	

Check the question that asks about cause and effect.

____ A. What happened after the water boiled?

____ B. How are the poem and the story alike?

____ C. What are the steps for sending an e-mail message?

You are correct if you checked A. It asks about the effect of boiling the water. *Alike* tells you to compare, so B is wrong. Answer C is wrong, because *the steps* are signal words for sequencing items.

Practice A: Match the cause and its effect. Write the letter on the line. Circle signal words.

_C_ 1. The electricity is out

___ 2. Ricardo broke his wrist;

___ 3. As a result of the vote,

___ 4. Leda always leaves at 7 o'clock

A. consequently, he can't play basketball.

B. so she gets to school on time.

C. (because) a tree fell on the power line.

D. Jin Lee is class president.

Practice B:

1. Write a cause to explain the effect. Use your own ideas. Use different signal words.

   Example: Alice borrows a library book every week _because she loves to read._

   _____ they arrived late.

2. Write an effect for the cause. Use your own ideas. Use signal words.

   Example: The senator agreed with the committee; _therefore, he voted for the bill._

   The store closes at 6 on Saturday _____

SEE PAGE 171 FOR ANSWERS.

Photocopying this page is prohibited by law.

Strategy 7 Understand Cause and Effect **41**

Writers don't put everything in a reading. Sometimes the reader has to **make an inference**, or guess, about the reading. This guess is also like drawing conclusions.

Roy's Room

Use *details* to make inferences: What can you tell about Roy?

Roy loves—   computers   nice clothes   baseball

There is a computer in Roy's room. There are clothes around his room, too. But there are many details about baseball. The best inference is *Roy loves baseball.*

Use *hints* to make inferences: How old is Roy?

Roy is—   4   14   24

There is no information about his age. But you can make an inference about it. This isn't a small child's room. It isn't an adult's room. There are many hints that a teenager lives there. The best inference is *Roy is 14.*

Read this conversation and make an inference about the boy and girl.

Boy: Excuse me. Is this Hunt Street?
Girl: No. Hunt Street is the next stop.
Boy: Thanks.

____ A. They are friends.

____ B. They are on a bus.

The answer is B. *Hint:* The girl talks about *the next stop*. They are probably on a bus. Answer A isn't true. Friends don't usually say *Excuse me* to ask a question.

Keys to Understanding

Signal Questions and Phrases: Making Inferences

Questions	Phrases
How do you know that . . . ? What *can you conclude* about . . . ? What *does it mean when* the narrator says . . . ? What *can you tell* about . . . ?	From the passage, the reader *can conclude* that . . . According to paragraph 8, you *can infer* that . . . In this paragraph, you *can tell* that . . .

Check the phrase that asks for an inference.

____ A. In paragraph 1, the narrator is unhappy because—

____ B. In paragraph 1, what is the first thing they see?

____ C. In paragraph 1, the reader can conclude—

You are correct if you checked C. It has the signal *conclude*. Answer A asks about cause and effect. It has the signal *because.* Answer B asks about sequence. It has the signal *first.*

Photocopying this page is prohibited by law.

Practice A: Good readers usually make many inferences. First, read the paragraph. Then, make your own inferences. Check *True* or *False*.

I do it every time! I go in for a quart of milk. I pick up a box of cereal. *Oh, look! There's a sale on yogurt.* I take five. Now I need a cart. *Hmmm. We're out of peanut butter. Manuel wants juice for his lunchbox, too.* Waiting in line, I grab a magazine. It goes into the cart. Finally, I escape. *Oh no! I forgot the milk!*

From this paragraph, you can tell that—	True	False
the speaker often shops this way.	✓	
1. the speaker is in a supermarket.		
2. Manuel is probably a cashier.		
3. the speaker has a shopping list.		
4. the speaker's thoughts are in italics.		

Practice B: Read the paragraphs below and on the next page. Answer the questions. Underline the parts that help you make an inference.

★★★★ *Orlo's Band* This funny movie is about <u>a group of teens</u>. <u>Their leader</u> is a ninth grader who <u>gets all his information from TV</u>.

What two things can you tell about Orlo?

___ A. He watches movies and plays in a band.

_✓_ B. He watches television and leads a band of kids.

1. Safety belts save lives. Be sure to wear both lap and shoulder belts. The lap belt should fit low and tight. The shoulder strap should cross the chest. Never slip the shoulder strap under your arm. That's very dangerous in cars with air bags.

What can you tell about some riders?

____ A. They always use seat belts.

____ B. They put shoulder belts under their arms.

2.

> TO: Parents of Math Club members
> FROM: Ms. Daly, Math Coach
>
> (1) On Friday, February 8, the Math Club is going to the Science Museum. (2) We will see a special show on number patterns. (3) Tickets are $2.00. (4) Please sign this permission slip and return it to me with $2.00 by Friday, February 1. (5) Parents who travel on the bus with the Math Club get free admission to the show.

From sentence 5, you can infer that Ms. Daly—

____ A. wants parents to ride on the bus with the students.

____ B. is driving the bus with students and parents on it.

3. My business grows continually. Every day, my life gets easier. My newspaper makes a lot of money. I am an example of the saying, "After getting your first $100, it's easier to get the second." Money makes money.[1]

What does the writer mean by this sentence?

> *After getting your first $100, it's easier to get the second.*

____ A. It's hard to start a new business. But once you do, it gets easier.

____ B. It's hard to stay successful. But it pays well.

SEE PAGE 171 FOR ANSWERS.

[1]Adapted from *The Autobiography of Benjamin Franklin, 1771.*

Photocopying this page is prohibited by law.

Distinguish Fact from Opinion

Good readers know the difference between **facts** and **opinions**.

Facts can be *proved*. Facts are *real information*. Names, places, data, and events are facts. Measures and weights are facts.

Opinions are what people *think* or *believe*. Opinions are about feelings or points of view.

Facts	Opinions
George Washington was *the first president* of the United States.	George Washington was a *great* president.
Multiplication is a *math operation*.	Multiplication is *easy*.
The sun *sets in the west*.	That's a *beautiful sunset*.
Independence Day is *July 4th*.	Independence Day is *my favorite holiday*.

Keys to Understanding

Signal Questions: Facts and Opinions

Facts	Opinions
Who was the first president of the United States?	Washington was a great president. *Agree or disagree.*
What kind of subject is multiplication?	Do you think multiplication is easy? *Why or why not?*
Where does the sun set?	*How* do you feel about the sunset?
When is Independence Day?	*Why* is Independence Day your favorite holiday?

Check the question that asks for a fact.

____ A. What is the temperature outside?

____ B. What winter sports are the best?

Answer A is correct. The temperature can be measured, so it is a fact. Answer B is an opinion. It asks you to compare with the signal *the best*.

Keys to Understanding

Signal Phrases: Opinion

I think . . .   I'd like/prefer . . .

You should . . .   He believes . . .

It's easy to see . . .   In my opinion . . .

It's clear that . . .   From my point of view . . .

Check the sentence that shows an opinion.

____ A. You must be 18 years old to vote in the United States.

____ B. I think 17-year-olds are smart enough to vote.

I think is a signal for opinion, so B is correct. The law says that voters must be 18 years old. So A is a fact.

Practice A: Check *Fact* or *Opinion.*

	Fact	Opinion
Why is paragraph 5 important?		✓
1. How does the author feel about global warming?		
2. Do you think grammar is fun?		
3. What evidence does the scientist give?		
4. Where is Vietnam?		
5. Why do you think the principal believes the boy?		
6. Who wrote the letter?		
7. Do you agree or disagree with this statement?		

SEE PAGE 171 FOR ANSWERS.

Practice B: Read the passages below. Each passage has several facts and one opinion. Underline the opinion. Circle any words that signal opinion.

Example: Grizzly bears weigh between 300 and 1500 pounds. They add about 400 more pounds for their winter's rest. They (should) eat less.

1. Tree frogs are a beautiful color. Their green color keeps them safe. An enemy can't see a green tree frog on a leaf.

2. Bats are nocturnal. They sleep during the day. They fly around at night. They eat many insects. I think bats are helpful.

3. Foxes are members of the dog family. Gray and red foxes live in the United States. They are cute and shy. Foxes live everywhere but Antarctica.

4. Army ants are nasty bugs. They have sharp stingers. They live in the rain forest.

5. Baby eagles are born tiny. But it's easy to see why they grow fast. They eat lots of fish and small birds.

Practice C: Read the topic. Write one opinion and one fact about the topic.

Topic: Many students study computers.

EXAMPLE

Your opinion: Everyone should learn to use computers.

Your fact: There are 20 computers in the lab.

Your opinion: _____

Your fact: _____

SEE PAGE 171 FOR ANSWERS.

Summarize and Paraphrase

Summarize: Find and describe the most important ideas in a passage. Ask: *What is this reading mostly about?*

Paraphrase: Retell the passage in your own words. First, read the passage. Then, describe what you remember about it. Put in main ideas and important details. Paraphrases are usually longer than summaries.

> My gerbils are great house pets. They are small and clean. They like to play with me. They like to play with each other, too. They aren't a lot of work. For example, you don't have to walk them three times a day.

Summary: My gerbils are great house pets for several reasons.

Paraphrase: My pet gerbils are great. They are clean, playful, and easy to care for.

Keys to Understanding

Signal Questions: Summarize and Paraphrase

Summarize	Paraphrase
Which saying best *summarizes* the . . . ?	Which is the best *restatement* of this sentence?
Which sentence from the reading *summarizes* the . . . ?	Which of the following is the best *restatement* of sentence 5?
What is the best *summary* of . . . ?	Another way *to state* sentence 15 is . . .
Choose the best *summary* of this article.	

Practice A: Read this story. Then check the correct answer.

Instruments by Size

Benny Goodman was a famous musician. A reporter once asked Benny's father why his son played the clarinet. Mr. Goodman wanted all his children to play an instrument. His oldest boy was big and strong, so he got a tuba, a big, heavy instrument. His middle son was average size, so he got a trumpet, a medium-sized instrument. The smallest son was Benny. He was ten years old. He got a clarinet, the lightest instrument. And he loved it!

1. What is the best summary of this article?

   ___ A. Mr. Goodman loved good music.

   ___ B. Mr. Goodman wanted Benny to play with his brothers.

   ___ C. Mr. Goodman liked to tell reporters about his children's music.

   ___ D. Mr. Goodman gave each son an instrument based on the boy's size.

2. Which is the best restatement of this sentence?

His oldest boy was big and strong, so he got a tuba, a big, heavy instrument.

   ___ A. A big, strong son needs a heavy tuba.

   ___ B. The oldest and strongest son got a big, heavy tuba.

   ___ C. The oldest son wanted to play a big, heavy instrument.

   ___ D. Only big, strong boys can play big, heavy instruments.

Practice B: Read the paragraph. Write a summary sentence and a paraphrase in your notebook.

Training

Zoovia and I want to run in the Boston Marathon. It is a 26-mile race. It goes through many towns near Boston. We train every day. We run in Natick and Framingham in the morning. We run in Ashland late at night. We run in Wellesley in the afternoon. We run in Boston on weekends. Soon we will run in Newton. That's the hardest part of the race. It's called Heartbreak Hill. Zoovia says, "After Heartbreak Hill, we will be ready for the marathon."

SEE PAGE 171 FOR ANSWERS.

CHAPTER 3: REVIEW TEST

Mark your answers on the Answer Grid.

Read this selection. Then answer Questions 1 through 8.

No one knows where or when the first kite was invented. But people generally think it was in ancient China. The kite probably followed trade routes around the world. Different cultures developed their own types and styles. But the basic scientific principle is the same. The flat, broad surface of the kite catches the wind and causes it to lift into the air, or fly.

To make a simple diamond-shaped paper kite, use the following materials:
- strong string or cord
- tape and glue
- sheet of strong paper, 40 inches by 40 inches
- 2 strong, straight wooden sticks or dowels

Step 1
Cut the sticks: Make one stick 40 inches long and the other one 35 inches long. Make cuts in the ends of both pieces of wood.

Step 2
Connect the sticks: Lay the long stick on a flat surface. Lay the short stick over the long stick, making a cross shape. Then use the string to tie the two sticks together where they meet. Make sure the sticks are at right angles. Then cover the string with glue. Let the glue dry.

Step 3
Make the frame: Run string around the outside of the frame, through the cuts in the sticks. Pull the string tight, but don't bend the sticks. Wrap the string several times around the top of the long stick. Cut it and tie it. This is the frame of the kite.

(Continued on next page)

GO ON

Step 4

Attach the paper: Lay the paper down on a flat surface and put the frame on top of it. Fold the edges of the paper over the frame and tape them in place. Then carefully remove the tape on one part of the frame at a time and glue the paper to the frame. Make sure everything is tight. Let the glue dry.

Step 5

Attach the string: Tie a loop of string to the back of the frame. Then attach the "flying string" to the loop. Tie another loop of string to the bottom of the frame and attach a ribbon. The ribbon, or tail, helps balance the kite.

Step 6

Have fun: Go outside and let your kite fly in the wind.

---

1 **What is the best title for this reading passage?**

   A Kite Building in Ancient China

   B Good Uses for Paper, String, and Glue

   C How to Build a Kite

   D Six Steps to a Great Activity

2 **The passage supports all the statements below, EXCEPT—**

   A kites can be made at home

   B kite flying is based on basic scientific principles

   C kites are popular in many cultures

   D toy makers took the kite to many places

3 **A kite flies because—**

   A the wind hits its broad, flat surface

   B paper is taped to wood

   C wind balances the ribbon, or tail, of the kite

   D the wind makes the sticks form right angles

4 **According to Step 2, the most important fact is—**

   A the flat surface needs to dry

   B the sticks must be made of special wood

   C the sticks have to be at right angles

   D the long stick has to be glued carefully

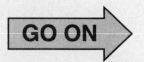
GO ON

5 From Step 4, you can infer that the tape holds the paper in place until you—

A   tie the sticks together

B   tie on the tail

C   lay the sticks down

D   glue the paper to the frame

6 What is the best restatement of Step 4?

A   Put the frame on the paper, so you can fold and tape the edges over it. Then, section by section, remove the tape and glue the paper to the frame.

B   Cover the sticks with paper. Glue them together and tape one stick at a time to the frame.

C   It's easy to keep the sticks at right angles to the paper. Then you can glue the string to the frame and tape the edges of the knots together.

D   Glue the paper tightly to the frame.

7 The last thing to do before you fly your kite is—

A   tie on the tail

B   tape a message to it

C   let all the string out

D   let the glue dry completely

8 What balances the kite?

A   the short stick

B   the flying string

C   the loops of string

D   the tail

The Spaghetti Harvest

1   Imagine you are watching a news program on television. A well-known reporter is telling the story. He is very serious. On the screen, a Swiss family picks real spaghetti off real trees and puts it into baskets.

2   The family looks happy. The mother tells the reporter that this is the biggest spaghetti crop in many years. No late frost ruined the flavor or made it hard to sell. The weather was perfect. There were no spaghetti weevils this year. "Before," she says, "those horrible insects ate the trees and ruined the pasta."

3   The reporter is curious. How can every strand of pasta be the same length? The father answers that they experimented for many years. Perfect spaghetti grows on perfect trees. They cut down the trees with spaghetti that is too short or too long.

4   At last, the reporter sits down to lunch at a table outside the farmhouse. He looks down at a plate of steaming, hot pasta with tomato sauce and smiles. "For those of you who love this dish," he tells the audience, "there's nothing like real, *home-grown* spaghetti."

5   "The Spaghetti Harvest" aired on British television on April 1, 1957. Many people forgot that it was April Fool's Day and believed the story was true. But it was a hoax.

6   After the show, there was a flood of calls to the TV station. Did spaghetti really grow on trees? The callers wanted to grow their own spaghetti. The people at the TV station kept the joke going. "Place a little bit of spaghetti in a can of tomato sauce and hope for the best," they said.

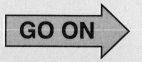

7   Not many people ate spaghetti in England in the 1950s. It was an unusual food then, and its origin was a mystery. The idea for the show came from a camera operator. His grade-school teacher said something he always remembered. She said, "You are so stupid! I'll bet you believe spaghetti grows on trees!"

8   This was one of the first hoaxes on television. Today, the story of the spaghetti harvest is number one on the list of the top 100 April Fool's Day hoaxes on the website of the Museum of Hoaxes.

9 **According to paragraph 2, the mother thinks that spaghetti weevils—**

  A   help the spaghetti crop

  B   are hard to sell

  C   are awful bugs

  D   add to the flavor of pasta

10 **The people in the Swiss family were probably—**

  A   actors

  B   farmers

  C   viewers

  D   reporters

11 **What is another way of writing the information in paragraph 6?**

  A   The TV station called a lot of viewers to tell them how to start spaghetti plants of their own.

  B   Many viewers called the TV station. They wanted to know how to grow their own spaghetti. The people at the station gave them a silly suggestion.

  C   The callers said there was a flood of tomato sauce on their spaghetti plants. They blamed the TV station.

  D   The TV station wanted to show callers how to grow their own spaghetti trees in a can with a little tomato sauce.

GO ON

12 **Which sentence is an opinion?**

   A April Fool's Day is April 1.

   B Not many people ate spaghetti in England in the 1950s.

   C You are so stupid!

   D This was one of the first hoaxes on television.

13 **What can you tell about April Fool's Day?**

   A It's a special pasta festival.

   B Reporters interview farmers.

   C People always forget it.

   D It's a day for jokes and tricks.

14 **Which is the best summary of "The Spaghetti Harvest"?**

   A In 1957, a reporter ate pasta on television and received many calls from viewers.

   B In 1957, a lot of people were fooled by a television show about growing spaghetti on trees.

   C In 1957, a camera operator proved to his teacher that spaghetti does grow on trees.

   D In 1957, a news program showed a Swiss family that grew pasta on their farm.

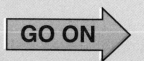

GO ON

Read this passage. Then answer questions 15 through 22.

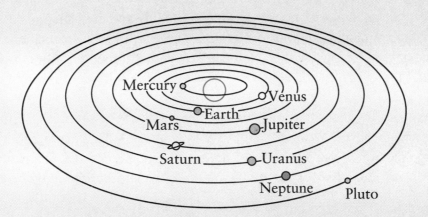

The Smallest Planet: Pluto

1 Pluto was discovered in 1930. It is the smallest planet in our solar system. It is only 1,430 miles (2,301 kilometers) across. That's about the distance from Dallas, Texas, to San Francisco, California.

2 Pluto has an odd orbit. It is usually the ninth planet from the sun. But not always. Sometimes it is closer to the sun than Neptune, the eighth planet. Every 248 years, the two planets change places. Then Pluto becomes the eighth planet for 20 years, while Neptune becomes the ninth planet. The next time this will happen is 2247. Don't forget to mark your calendar!

3 When Pluto is closest to the sun, it is still 2.7 billion miles (4.34 billion km) away. When it is farthest from the sun, it is 4.6 billion miles (7.4 billion km) away. Pluto is so small and so far away that you always need a telescope to see it from Earth. Even then, the planet named for the Roman god of the underworld looks like a dim dot of light.

4 There are other interesting facts about the planet. For example, Pluto rotates in the opposite direction from most other planets. Your weight on Pluto would be only 1/15 what it is on Earth. That's great for pole-vaulting or playing basketball if you get there. But you can't. It is just too far away. Pluto, like Neptune and Jupiter, is too cold for you to play anything anyway. The average temperature on Pluto's surface is $-378°$ to $-396°$ Fahrenheit ($-228°$ to $-238°$ Celsius).

(Continued on next page)

5   Scientists think that Pluto is made up mostly of frozen nitrogen and rocks. But when the planet gets close to the sun, it "warms up." The ice begins to melt a little. It forms an atmosphere. The atmosphere is nitrogen gas with some carbon monoxide and methane mixed in.

6   Pluto has one moon named Charon. In Greek mythology, Charon steers the ferry that brings dead souls to the underworld. Charon doesn't act like a normal moon. It doesn't just go around Pluto. Charon and Pluto go around each other! Charon is a very big moon compared to its planet. It is about half as big as Pluto.

7   Some astronomers say that Pluto isn't a real planet at all. They say it is too small. It is just half the size of Mercury. It is even smaller than other moons in the solar system, including our own. But an important organization of astronomers declared that Pluto should still be counted as a planet. Pluto's fans are happy. Now they can still say that Pluto is their favorite *planet*.

---

15 **Which sentence BEST sums up paragraph 2?**

A   Pluto has an odd orbit.

B   Every 248 years Pluto and Neptune change places.

C   The next time Pluto will be the ninth planet from the sun is 2247.

D   When Pluto is closest to the sun, it is still 2.7 billion miles (4.34 billion km) away.

16 **From paragraph 3, you can conclude that the ancient Romans believed the god Pluto—**

A   followed the sun

B   made telescopes

C   lived in a dark place

D   had dots

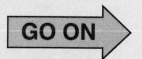

17 **What is the best restatement of this sentence?**

> Pluto is so small and so far away that you always need a telescope to see it from Earth.

A Pluto is an invisible planet.

B Pluto is always invisible from Earth.

C You need a telescope to see all small planets like Pluto.

D Pluto is invisible from Earth without a telescope.

18 **Pluto is different from most other planets in the solar system because it—**

A is cold

B rotates in the opposite direction

C moves around the sun

D has only one moon

19 **Your weight on Pluto is—**

A more than it is on Earth

B less than it is on Earth

C good for pole-vaulting

D about the same as on Earth

20 **Sometimes Pluto's ice melts. This effect happens when—**

A its nitrogen freezes

B it's closest to the sun

C it forms an atmosphere

D carbon monoxide and methane mix with nitrogen

21 **Some astronomers did not want Pluto to be called a planet because—**

A it's smaller than Charon

B they only want eight planets in the solar system

C planets must be smaller than their moons

D Pluto is much smaller than Mercury

22 **Choose the best summary of paragraph 7.**

A Pluto isn't a real planet.

B Pluto is smaller than Mercury.

C Astronomers finally agree that Pluto is a real planet.

D Pluto's fans are glad it's a planet.

**STOP. THIS IS THE END OF THE REVIEW TEST.
SEE PAGE 171 FOR ANSWERS AND EXPLANATIONS.**

Build Literary Skills

Recognize Figurative Language

Figurative Language

- forms a picture or image in the reader's mind

- uses the five senses (sight, hearing, taste, touch, or smell) to show an idea

- compares things or ideas

Writers use figurative language to make a reading more interesting. Three kinds of figurative language are personification, similes, and metaphors.

1. **Personification** shows human feelings or actions in animals or things.

The **sun smiles** in the morning.

The sun doesn't really smile. But readers understand that a "smiling" sun means good feelings or nice weather.

2. **Similes** use **like** or **as** to compare.

He is **as** slow **as** a **turtle**.

The sentence compares a slow runner to a turtle. It is a simile because it uses the word *as*.

3. **Metaphors** compare two things without *like* or *as*. Metaphors compare by saying one thing **is** the other.

The **girl is** a real **songbird**.

The metaphor says the good singer *is* a songbird.

Write *personification*, *simile*, or *metaphor*.

Example: <u>metaphor</u> He's a clown.

————————— A. The wind tickles the trees.

————————— B. Efram is a hurricane of movement.

————————— C. Marianna's eyes are like diamonds.

Answer A is personification. People tickle things. But when you say the wind tickles the trees, you know the wind is gentle. Answer B is a metaphor. Hurricanes move fast, so you can tell how Efram moves. Answer C is a simile. It compares Marianna's eyes to sparkling diamonds. It's a simile because it uses *like*.

Practice: Find the figurative language in the excerpts below. Check **P** for personification, **S** for simile, or **M** for metaphor. Then complete the sentences. Explain what the author compares or personifies. Last, write what you think the author means by the figurative language.

	P	S	M
The principal looked as tall as a skyscraper.		✓	
The author *compares the principal to a skyscraper.*			
I think *the principal is tall and a little scary.*			
1. The brakes squealed, and the train groaned to a stop.			
The author _____			
I think _____			
2. He was a tall, lanky young man with long arms and legs . . . and feet like shovels.[1]			
The author _____			
I think _____			
3. Dear March, come in! How glad I am! I looked for you before. Put down your hat— You must have walked— How out of breath you are![2]			
The poet _____			
I think _____			
4. Alice is a rose, complete with thorns.			
The poet _____			
I think _____			

SEE PAGE 173 FOR ANSWERS.

[1] From Washington Irving, *The Legend of Sleepy Hollow.*
[2] From Emily Dickinson, "Dear March, come in!"

Analyze Characters and Recognize Point of View

Analyze Characters

Characters are people or animals in a story. Characters have personality, feelings, and ideas. They can be real or made-up.

Writers tell you about a story's characters through:

descriptions: how the characters look, what they do, how they think
quotations: what the characters say

Writers also want you to understand characters' **motivation**, or the reasons they act the way they do.

 # Keys to Understanding

Signal Questions: Character's Motivation

Why does the character do . . . ?
Why doesn't the character do . . . ?
What makes a character decide to . . . ?

Read about these four girls. They all work in the library after school. But each girl has a different motivation.

Dewi uses her money for drum lessons. Momoko puts her money in a jar at home. Aida puts her money in a college fund. Jo buys nice clothes.

Write a name next to each girl's motivation.

Example: _Momoko_ wants to buy her brother a nice present.

A. —————— wants to be a doctor.

B. —————— wants to look good.

C. —————— wants to play in the school band.

Aida is A. She knows it costs a lot to be a doctor. Jo is B. She buys nice clothes because they make her look good. Dewi is C. She needs drum lessons.

TIP

Information between quotations marks ("**I Love NY!**") does not show point of view.

Point of view is how the narrator sees and tells the story. The character telling a story is the narrator. Each narrator has a point of view. A narrator in the story uses the first-person point of view. A narrator outside the story uses the third-person point of view.

Keys to Understanding

Point of View

First-person point of view: The narrator is a character *in* the story.

I is the character telling this story. This narrator knows the story from only one point of view.

Texts that use first-person point of view: autobiography, personal narrative, general fiction

Signals: *I, me, my, we, us, our*	*I* was scared even though Ilya was with *me*. It was dark and *my* flashlight didn't work. *We* tried to walk carefully through the woods, but several branches slapped *us* as we passed. Soon *our* arms and faces were covered with cuts.

Third-person point of view: The narrator is *outside* the story.

The narrator has no name. He or she knows everything about the story from the outside.

Texts that use third-person point of view: biography, informational texts, general fiction

Signals: *her, them, she, he, they, him, it*	Juanita asked *her* grandfather to help *them*. *She* knew that *he* always baked the holiday bread. Together, the two girls and the old man made the special loaf. Then *they* helped *him* lift *it* into the hot oven.

Check the sentence with a first-person point of view.

____ A. The words washed over them like the sea.

____ B. We always have a barbecue on Independence Day.

The signal *We* tells you B is a first-person point of view. In A, the signal *them* shows a third-person point of view. (Do you see the simile in A?)

Practice A: Review some readings in this book. Complete this chart.

Reading	Signals	Point of View	
		1st person	3rd person
My Ántonia p. 6	I, my, we	✓	
1. "Vietnam's Math Prizes for Girls," p. 22			
2. "Frankenstein," p. 38			
3. "Training," p. 50			
4. "The Spaghetti Harvest," p. 54			
5. "Dear March, come in!" p. 63			

Practice B: Review some readings in this book. What can you tell about these characters? Check the best answers.

1. What can you tell about Jamal Qualls? (from "Students Join Firefighters for Burned Children," p. 2)

—— A. He is a leader.

—— B. He is tall for his age.

—— C. He wants to be a firefighter.

2. What is Maria Gomez like? (from "Seeing Triple," p. 24)

—— A. She's shy.

—— B. She's lonely.

—— C. She outgoing.

3. What words best describe Maya Lin? (from "Biography Note: Maya Lin," p. 35)

—— A. hostile and angry

—— B. hardworking and determined

—— C. relaxed and cautious

4. Benny Goodman's father— (from "Instruments by Size," p. 50)

—— A. was a musician

—— B. loved music

—— C. loved his oldest son best

SEE PAGE 173 FOR ANSWERS.

Recognize Setting, Plot, and Problem Resolution

Setting: the time and place of a story. The setting can be in the past, present, or future. The place can be real or imaginary.

I was born <u>on May 14, 1956, in Beijing, China</u>.
Margaret Johnson is graduating from Space School on <u>Saturday, April 3.</u> Come celebrate with us <u>from 5 p.m. to 8 p.m. at the Solar Inn, the Space Station, Mars.</u>
"<u>At that time</u>," continued the Wizard, "there were <u>four separate countries in this Land</u>. I ordered the Emerald City to be built just <u>where the four countries cornered together</u> . . ."[3]

Plot: what happens in a story. Plots usually follow a sequence.

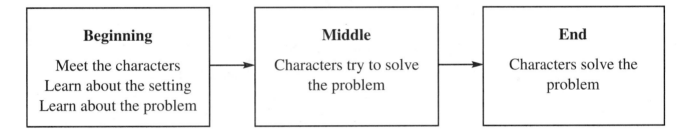

Beginning	**Middle**	**End**
Meet the characters Learn about the setting Learn about the problem	Characters try to solve the problem	Characters solve the problem

Problem resolution: outcomes or conclusions. Characters often have a struggle or problem. The resolution is how the problem is solved.

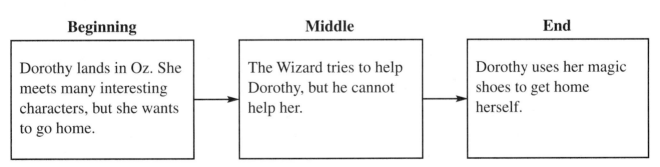

Beginning	**Middle**	**End**
Dorothy lands in Oz. She meets many interesting characters, but she wants to go home.	The Wizard tries to help Dorothy, but he cannot help her.	Dorothy uses her magic shoes to get home herself.

[3] From L. Frank Baum, *Dorothy and the Wizard of Oz.*

Read the story. Complete the chart. Write *Setting, Problem,* or *Resolution*.

The Woodcutter's Children

Once upon a time, a woodcutter lived with his children near a forest. One day, a witch took the children. She hid them in her house in the forest. The witch planned to eat them. They ran away, but the witch soon found them. They hit her with a stone and killed her.

The woodcutter looked for his children all day and all night. Finally he found the witch's house. His children were safe inside. The family was together and happy again.

---

characters	A. _____	B. _____	C. _____
children woodcutter witch	The children kill the witch.	Once upon a time near a forest	The witch wants to eat the children.

A is the resolution. The children kill the witch to save themselves. B is the setting. It tells the time and place of the story. C is the problem.

Keys to Understanding

Signal Questions: Setting, Plot, and Problem Resolution

Setting	Time	When does the story happen? In what year do the events take place? What is the time/date of the story?
	Place	Where does the story take place? In what town/city/country are the characters?
Plot		What happens first/next/last?
Problem Resolution		What choice does the main character make? How is the problem solved? What does a character do to fix the problem?

Check the sentence about problem resolution.

___ A. Next, the boy goes down to the water.

___ B. The boy decides to fix the boat himself.

___ C. The boy lives near the Gulf of Mexico.

Answer B is correct. The word *decides* shows that the boy makes a choice. *Next* in A is a sequence word. It answers a question about the plot. Answer C answers a question about setting: *Where.*

Practice A: Read this paragraph. Answer the questions.

(1) The new machines on his Ohio farm let Jesse Bentley do more work with fewer workers. (2) But farming didn't make him happy. (3) Jesse had grown up in America after the Civil War. (4) Like other men of his time, he was influenced by modern industry. (5) Jesse always wanted more. (6) He might stop farming altogether. (7) He'd open a factory and make machines instead.[4]

1. The setting is described in sentences __1__ and _____.

2. The problem is described in sentences _____ and _____.

3. The resolution is described in sentences _____ and _____.

Practice B: Read the fable. Answer the questions. Use sentences in the story or your own words.

The Lion and the Mouse

One day a mouse ran over a lion's face. The lion woke up and roared in anger. He grabbed the mouse by her tail.

"Please forgive me, Lion," begged the mouse. "Please let me go. I will help you one day!" The lion laughed. "You will help me! That's funny." The lion let the mouse go free because she made him laugh.

Soon some hunters caught the lion and tied him with strong ropes. Again, the lion roared in anger. The mouse heard his cry. She came to see what was wrong. She chewed the rope with her sharp little teeth and set the lion free.

"You didn't believe I could ever help you. Now you see, even the smallest creature can sometimes be as strong as a lion."

Example: This story's setting is in the jungle. How can you tell?
The characters are jungle animals. Hunters catch the lion.

1. What is the lion's problem? _____

    _____

2. What does the mouse do to solve the problem? _____

    _____

SEE PAGE 173 FOR ANSWERS.

[4] Adapted from Sherwood Anderson, *Winesburg, Ohio*.

Recognize Mood, Foreshadowing, Flashback, and Imagery

Mood: the *feeling* a reader gets from a story or poem. Some moods are happy, sad, or angry.

Here are two parts of Edgar Allen Poe's poem "The Bells."

II.	IV.
Hear the **mellow wedding** bells, **Golden** bells! What a world of **happiness** their **harmony** foretells!	Hear the **tolling** of the bells, **Iron** bells! What a world of **solemn** thought their melody compels!

Part II: The words *mellow*, *wedding*, *golden*, *happiness*, and *harmony* show a happy mood.

Part IV: This part uses sad words. Bells *toll*, or ring, for the dead. The golden bells are now *iron*. Instead of happiness, the world is *solemn*, or sad.

Foreshadowing: a clue or hint about an event to come later in the story. Foreshadowing helps you guess what may happen. It helps you make predictions, too.

Read this part of "The Red-Headed League." Mr. Wilson is talking to Sherlock Holmes, the detective. Wilson is describing an employee named Spaulding.

"Spaulding is a good worker. He wants to learn the business. So he works for half-pay. But he has his faults," said Mr. Wilson. "Always with his hobby—photography. Snapping away with a camera, then running down to the cellar to develop his pictures."

Sherlock Holmes is a good detective. He always looks for clues:

Most good workers don't work for half-pay.
They don't take a lot of pictures at work.
They don't go down to the cellar all the time.

Like detectives, good readers use foreshadowing to make predictions about what Spaulding may do.

[5] Adapted from Sir Arthur Conan Doyle, *The Adventures of Sherlock Holmes*.

Check the sentence that shows mood.

_____ A. We didn't know where Arno lived. But he had a Texas driver's license.

_____ B. The sun sparkles in the river. The day is new, and the air is sweet.

Answer B is correct. It uses positive, upbeat words to show a good mood. Answer A shows foreshadowing. His Texas driver's license is a clue.

Flashback: an event that happened _before_ the story starts. Writers often put flashbacks in the middle of a story. Flashbacks help explain the present. Movies often use flashbacks, too.

Read this story. Think about which paragraphs show a flashback.

1   "I want to get Dad a nice birthday present," Ali tells his mother. "But I don't have any money."

2   "Why don't you _do_ something nice for him, instead?" suggests Mom. "He'd like that. And it won't cost anything."

3   Ali thinks about a conversation he had with his father last Saturday. They were driving to soccer practice.

4   "This car looks bad. I wish it was clean!" Dad said. "But I never have time to wash it. It just sits outside and gets dirty."

5   Ali gets up early on his father's birthday. He cleans the inside of the car. He washes the outside. He scrubs everything until it shines. Then he puts a big bow on the roof.

6   His father loves his birthday present!

Paragraphs 1, 2, 5, and 6 happen in the present. They happen in sequence, too. Paragraphs 3 and 4 tell about events that happened _before_ the rest of the story. They are a flashback.

Keys to Understanding

Signal Words: Flashbacks

Time words about the past: *last* Saturday, *before* school, *during* the snowstorm

Past tense verbs in present tense stories:

Present	Past
Ali says . . .	Ali said . . .
Dad is driving.	Dad was driving.

Imagery: Mental pictures. Imagery helps make pictures in your mind. It uses the five senses—sight, taste, touch, hearing, and smell. Imagery reminds you of how something looks, tastes, feels, sounds, or smells. Imagery is often used in poetry.

Deep-hearted, pure, with
scented dew still wet—
One perfect rose[6]

Doctor Harry spread a warm
paw like a cushion on her
forehead . . .[7]

The fog comes in on little
cat feet[8]

Check the two senses this image uses.

A crack of thunder. Red wings flash.

—— sight —— taste —— touch —— hearing —— smell

The two senses are hearing and sight. *A crack of thunder* is a sound, so you use your hearing. *Red wings flash* is a colorful picture. You use your sight.

[6] From Dorothy Parker, "One Perfect Rose."
[7] From Katherine Ann Porter, "The Jilting of Granny Weatherall."
[8] From Carl Sandburg, "The Fog."

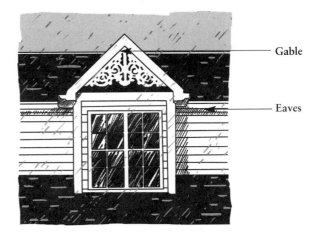

Gable

Eaves

Practice A: Read this excerpt from "Summer Shower" by Emily Dickinson. (*Eaves* and *gables* are parts of a roof.) Complete the sentences.

> A drop fell on the apple tree,
> Another on the roof;
> A half a dozen kissed the eaves,
> And made the gables laugh.

Example: A figure of speech used in this poem is <u>personification.</u>

1. The mood of this poem is _____.

2. One word from the poem that shows this mood is _____.

3. I see an image of _____ from this poem.

4. A word or phrase from the poem that gives me this image is

   _____.

5. I use my sense(s) of _____ to understand this image.

Photocopying this page is prohibited by law.

All the Way Home

"Fernanda, why do you take Dusty everywhere you go?" asks Luis. Fernanda takes her dog, Dusty, shopping. She takes him on trips. She even takes Dusty to the doctor's office for her checkups! Dusty is a nice dog. But Luis thinks Fernanda forgets that Dusty is just a dog.

"Dusty goes with me because he's my best friend," Fernanda answers. "Let me tell you a story about him."

One day Fernanda got very sick. She went to the hospital. Her son, José, put the dog in the yard. Dusty waited for Fernanda, but she didn't come home. So the dog jumped over the fence.

Dusty found the hospital somehow. He stood in front and barked and howled. Fernanda was asleep in her room. Her window was closed. She didn't hear Dusty barking outside. A hospital guard called the dogcatcher.

The guard said, "Come and take this stray dog away."

José called Fernanda that night. "Dusty is lost, Mom," he said. "I'm very sorry."

The next day Fernanda left the hospital. She was very sad. Suddenly, a dog ran down the street. A dogcatcher ran after him. The dogcatcher yelled to Fernanda. "Grab that dog. It ran away from the pound!"

"That was my Dusty," says Fernanda, smiling. "He jumped into my arms. He did everything to find me. Now nothing can stop me from keeping Dusty close!"

	Foreshadowing	Flashback
A hospital guard called the dog pound.	✓	
1. "Dusty goes with me because he's my best friend," Fernanda answers.		
2. The next day Fernanda left the hospital .		
3. One day Fernanda got very sick.		
4. She even takes Dusty to the doctor's office for her checkups!		

SEE PAGE 173 FOR ANSWERS.

Photocopying this page is prohibited by law.

Strategy 15

Identify Theme and Author's Purpose

Theme: the central idea or lesson of a story. Themes are important ideas or meanings in a writing.

Here are some general themes in literature:

- relationships with family or friends

- feelings such as love or hate, or being kind or selfish

- the difficulty of growing up, including making decisions and taking responsibility

- keeping traditions or learning new ways

- learning what is true or important and what is not

Read this paragraph. Think about the themes above as you read.

An old man named Ebenezer Scrooge hears his nephew, Fred, talk about him.

"I feel sorry for him," says Fred. "After all, who gets hurt when he's mean? He does! Here's an example. He decided he didn't like us. So he refused to come to our house. And what's the result? He lost out on a really good dinner. See—he is the one who suffers."[9]

This paragraph hints at several themes: family relationships, being kind or selfish, and learning what is important and what is not.

 Keys to Understanding

Signal Questions: Theme

What is the *main theme* of the passage?
What is the *importance* of Fred's description of his uncle?
What is the *result* of Scrooge refusing to visit his nephew?
What can you *learn from* Scrooge's actions?
What *message* does the author want to give?
Which best describes the *central idea* of this passage?

[9] Adapted from Charles Dickens, *A Christmas Carol*.

Author's Purpose: the reason for writing a poem, story, article, or book.

Authors often write to—

- **Inform or explain**. An author gives facts or makes information clear. Informational texts are nonfiction.

  Example texts: history, science, news stories, how-to articles, interviews

- **Persuade or influence**. An author gives advice, wants to change your mind, or asks you to do something. Persuasive writing often shows the positive or negative sides (the pros or cons) of a topic.

  Example texts: letters to the editor, editorials, advertisements, speeches

- **Narrate or express**. An author tells a story or writes about feelings or ideas.

  Example texts: novels, poems, short stories, personal narratives, folktales, diaries, plays

- **Entertain**. The author wants to make you laugh or smile. Readings that entertain can be funny, silly, or scary.

  Example texts: science fiction, mysteries, comic novels, limericks, ghost stories, jokes

This is a special poem called a limerick. Read it. Then check the author's purpose.

There once was a short girl in 6th grade.
Basketball was the game she played.
She dribbled and passed,
She ran, and at last,
She jumped and the winning shot made.

The author's purpose is to—

—— A. inform   —— C. narrate

—— B. persuade   —— D. entertain

You are correct if you checked D. Limericks are funny poems. Limerick writers usually want to entertain.

Keys to Understanding

Signal Questions: Author's Purpose

What is the narrator's *main purpose* in this passage?

What does the writer *want you to do*?

What was the author's *reason for writing* this passage?

The information in this article *is mainly intended to*…

The author probably *wrote this story to*…

Practice: Read the passages below and on the next page. Then check the correct answer.

TO THE EDITOR:

Your article about Front Street Park didn't show the whole picture. Some people say the park is ugly. There is garbage everywhere. There are no bushes or flowers or grass. And there is no money to improve it.

The mayor says, "It's time to sell the land and turn it into a parking lot." But I remember a very different park. It was clean and beautiful 20 years ago. Children played there. Parents watched their kids and talked to each other. We don't need much money to fix it. Why can't we get together and clean up the park ourselves? Why can't we plant bushes and flowers and grass ourselves? The park may be ugly now, but next year it could be beautiful again!

Sincerely,
Rodrigo Velez

1. Mr. Velez's purpose is to—

____A. narrate

____B. influence

____C. entertain

2. What is his main theme?

____A. Parks take a lot of money to keep clean.

____B. People can work together to make a park beautiful again.

____C. Families need good places to meet and play.

Photocopying this page is prohibited by law.

Valentine cards first became popular around 200 years ago. Cards were painted by hand. They had silk ribbons or flowers made of feathers. Others smelled of perfume. But those valentines were expensive. Later, cards were made by machine. They were much cheaper. Those ribbons and flowers were printed instead. They looked like the cards we send today.

3. The author's purpose is to—

——A. inform

——B. persuade

——C. express

4. What is the central idea of this paragraph?

——A. Sending cards on Valentine's Day is an old tradition.

——B. Handmade items are more beautiful but more expensive than machine-made ones.

——C. Old Valentine cards have silk ribbons, feather flowers, and smell good.

A man from England visited an American friend after the American Revolution. He wanted to meet George Washington.

The president was across the street a short time later. "There he goes," the American said.

"Is that really George Washington?" the Englishman asked. "Where are his guards? Where are the soldiers to protect him from the people?"

"They are all around you," the American said proudly. He pointed to everyone on the street. He pointed to himself. "President Washington is the president of all the people."

5. The author's purpose is to—

——A. entertain

——B. persuade

——C. narrate

6. What message does the author want you to get?

——A. English visitors to America can meet the president.

——B. The president of a free country doesn't have to be afraid of its citizens.

——C. George Washington didn't want the Secret Service to guard him.

SEE PAGE 174 FOR ANSWERS.

Mark your answers on the Answer Grid.

Read this story. Then answer Questions 1 through 9.

The Necklace[10]

1   Mathilde and her husband were invited to a fancy ball. Mathilde wanted to look beautiful. She borrowed a diamond necklace from her rich friend, Jeanne. But then Mathilde lost the necklace. She and her husband bought a diamond necklace that looked just like it. The new necklace was very expensive. Mathilde and her husband borrowed a lot of money to pay for the necklace. They never told Jeanne what happened. They just gave her the new necklace and pretended it was the old one.

2   Mathilde and her husband worked for ten years to pay off their debt. Finally, they were done. But Mathilde looked much older. Sometimes she sat down by the window and remembered when she was beautiful. How quickly life changes. It takes only one thing.

3   One Sunday Mathilde saw Jeanne in a park. Jeanne still looked beautiful. Mathilde went over to her and said hello. Jeanne did not recognize her.

4   "You're making a mistake," said Jeanne. "I don't know you."

5   "I am Mathilde Loisel."

6   Her old friend Jeanne cried out. "Oh, my poor Mathilde! You've changed so much."

7   "Yes. Life was very hard," said Mathilde. "And it was because of you."

8   Jeanne was surprised. "Because of me? What do you mean?"

9   "Do you remember that diamond necklace that you lent me for the ball?" asked Mathilde. "Well, I lost it."

10 "How can that be? You brought it back to me."

11 "I brought you back another necklace just like it. We borrowed the money to pay for it. It took ten years to pay off our debt. That wasn't easy for us." Mathilde was very proud. "You didn't notice that the necklace was different, did you?"

12 "You bought a diamond necklace to replace mine?" asked Jeanne. She took Mathilde by both hands. "Oh, my poor Mathilde. Those diamonds were fake! They were worthless!"

[10] Adapted from Guy de Maupassant, "The Necklace."

Photocopying this page is prohibited by law.

1   Read the sentences.

> Mathilde and her husband borrowed a lot of money to pay for the necklace. They never told Jeanne what happened. They just gave her the new necklace and pretended it was the old one.

This is an example of—

A   flashback

B   foreshadowing

C   imagery

D   problem resolution

2

Why doesn't Mathilde tell Jeanne the necklace was lost?

A   Jeanne's friendship is important to her.

B   Mathilde enjoys hard work.

C   Mathilde is too proud to admit her problem.

D   Mathilde is afraid of Jeanne.

3   In paragraph 2, the author creates a mood that is—

A   angry

B   lighthearted

C   cheerful

D   sad

4   Jeanne doesn't recognize Mathilde because—

A   Mathilde looks much older

B   Jeanne's sight is poor

C   Jeanne is too vain to notice her old friend

D   Mathilde is wearing old clothes

5   In paragraph 7, you can tell that Mathilde—

A   blames Jeanne for her hard life

B   is ashamed that she looks old

C   feels responsible for her problems

D   doesn't worry about the past

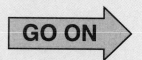
GO ON

6 The author's use of third-person point of view helps the reader understand—

A why Mathilde borrowed a necklace

B how she changed in 10 years

C Jeanne's attitude about her necklace

D all of the above

7 What is the narrator's main purpose in this passage?

A to entertain readers with a funny ending

B to persuade readers not to borrow jewelry

C to inform readers about fake jewels

D to tell a story about making a big mistake

8 Which saying BEST summarizes the author's main message?

A Don't be a borrower or a lender.

B False pride costs a lot.

C You are never too old to learn.

D Time heals all wounds.

9 Which sentence describes part of the plot?

A The main character makes a choice.

B The characters meet in the park.

C The story is in the third-person point of view.

D The story has a surprise ending.

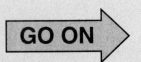
GO ON

The Weather of New England[11]

I think there must be a factory here where trainee weathermen practice making weather for the rest of the world. They experiment by making weather in New England first. The weather here is always doing something different. Last spring I counted 136 different kinds of weather in one day.

I met a man preparing a weather exhibit. He was going to travel around the world to collect weather. I said, "Don't do it. Just come to New England." Well, he came here and got his collection in four days. He discovered weathers that he had never heard of before. He had more weather than he needed. He had weather to sell; weather to invest; weather to give to the poor. Everyone thought the exhibit was a great success.

Now, pity the poor man who tries to predict the weather here. New England forecasts start something like this: "Probable northeast to southwest winds will vary westward and eastward and all points in between. Expect high and low pressure readings with areas of rain, snow, hail, and drought. That will be succeeded or preceded by earthquakes, with thunder and lightning." Forecasts often end, "But it is possible that all this may completely change by tomorrow."

[11] Adapted from Mark Twain's speech at the New England Society's 71st Annual Dinner, December 22, 1876.

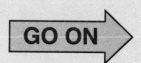

10 This speech is written—

A from the first-person point of view

B as a flashback

C with an interesting plot

D in a serious mood

11 Which sentence from the speech is an example of problem resolution?

A I think there must be a factory where trainee weathermen practice making weather for the rest of the world.

B I met a man preparing a weather exhibit.

C Well, he came here and got his collection in four days.

D Everyone thought the exhibit was a great success.

12 The speaker's purpose in this speech is to—

A collect

B entertain

C influence

D inform

13 Which saying BEST describes the central message of this speech?

A Red sky at night, sailor's delight. Red sky in the morning, sailor take warning.

B If you don't like New England's weather, wait ten minutes.

C Wind in the west, weather is best.

D It never rains, it pours.

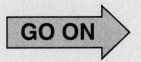

Columbus[12]

(1) They sailed. They sailed. Then spake[13] the mate:
     "This mad sea shows his teeth to-night.
     He curls his lip, he lies in wait,
(4) With lifted teeth, as if to bite!
     Brave Admiral, say but one good word:
     What shall we do when hope is gone?"
     The words leapt like a leaping sword:
(8) "Sail on! sail on! sail on! and on!"
     Then, pale and worn, he kept his deck,
     And looked through darkness. Ah, that night
     Of all dark nights! And then a speck—
(12) A light! A light! A light! A light!
     It grew, a starlit flag unfurled!
     It grew to be Time's burst of dawn.
     He gained a world; he gave that world
(16) Its grandest lesson: "On! sail on!"

14 **Lines 1 through 6 are mainly about—**

A a large sea creature

B the mate's fear and lack of hope

C the Admiral's directions and language

D the danger of a "leaping sword"

15 **What word describes the mood of the sea in lines 2 to 4?**

A peaceful

B calm

C dangerous

D lonely

---

[12] From Joachim Miller, "Columbus."
[13] *spake* is an old way of saying *said.*

16 Who is the "Brave Admiral?"

    A the mate

    B Columbus

    C the mad sea

    D the sword

17 The setting of the poem is important because it helps the reader understand—

    A how far Columbus sailed

    B why Columbus tried to find another land

    C the number of days Columbus and his crew sailed

    D the dangers Columbus and his mate faced

18 Which lines from the poem use personification, the literary technique that gives objects or things human qualities?

    A They sailed. They sailed.

    B This mad sea shows his teeth to-night. / He curls his lip, he lies in wait, / With lifted teeth, as if to bite!

    C Then, pale and worn, he kept his deck, / And looked through darkness.

    D He gained a world; he gave that world / Its grandest lesson: "On! sail on!"

19 Read this portion of the poem.

> Ah, that night
> Of all dark nights! And then a speck— A light! A light! A light! A light!
> It grew, a starlit flag unfurled!

This is an example of the poet's use of—

    A flashback

    B imagery

    C simile

    D plot

20 Another way to express the poet's theme as stated in line 16 is—

    A All hands on deck!

    B Beware sea monsters!

    C Don't give up!

    D Land ahead!

STOP. THIS IS THE END OF THE REVIEW TEST.
SEE PAGE 175 FOR ANSWERS AND EXPLANATIONS.

Chapter 5

Build Vocabulary Skills

Make Analogies

Identifying an Analogy

An **analogy** is a relationship, or connection, between word pairs. Analogies can help you figure out new words by comparing them to words you know. On some tests, an analogy has **a stem pair** and **answer pairs**. On other tests, an analogy is **in a sentence**.

An analogy stem

looks like this: BIRD : NEST

reads like this: *bird **is to** nest*

On tests, you have to find the connection between the stem pair and an answer pair. Read the test analogy about a creature and its home.

A test analogy stem and answer choices

look like this: BIRD : NEST ::   { stem pair
            A. fly : home
            B. dog : run
            C. bee : hive ✓   } answer pairs
            D. animal : pet

read like this: *bird is to nest **as** bee is to hive*

A bird lives in a nest. Look for a pair with a similar relationship. The answer pair that is similar is *A bee lives in a hive.*

Keys to Understanding

Strategies to Solve a Test Analogy

Step 1 Figure out the connection between the words in the stem.

Step 2 Think of a bridge sentence.

Step 3 Test the answer choices in your bridge sentence.

Step 4 Use the process of elimination[1] if needed.

Solving a Test Analogy

Step 1 Figure out the **connection** between the words in the stem.

There are many ways word pairs can be connected.

The stem can be:
a part and a whole

FINGER : HAND

a person and what he/she does

SKATER : SPINS

two opposites

SUN : MOON

a thing and what it does

SWITCH : LIGHT

an action and what happens
because of the action

KICK : SCORE

different words with similar
meanings

BOAT : SHIP

[1] Information on the process of elimination is in Chapter 1, pages 17–19.

Step 2 Think of a **bridge sentence**.

Make a **bridge sentence**. A good bridge sentence shows the special relationship or connection between the first pair of words. Bridge sentences are short, but helpful.

Analogy	Bridge
DRINK : GLASS	You drink from a glass.

The bridge connects an action (drink) with what you need for that action (glass).

Compare these **weak** and **strong** bridges.

Analogy	Weak Bridge	Strong Bridge
MONEY : BANK	Money is in a bank.	You save money in a bank.

Money is in a bank is a weak bridge. Money is in other places, too. It doesn't show a special connection. *You save money in a bank* is a strong bridge. It shows a special action.

Analogy	Weak Bridge	Strong Bridge
TALL : SHORT	A child can be tall or short.	Tall is the opposite of short.

The sentence *A child can be tall or short* doesn't show the difference clearly. The phrase *is the opposite of* shows exactly how the words are related.

Analogy	Weak Bridge	Strong Bridge
LEG : KNEE	I have a leg and a knee.	A leg bends at the knee.

I have a leg and a knee is too general. You have other body parts, too. It doesn't show the special connection between the two words.
A leg bends at the knee shows two important connections:
(1) a whole-to-part relationship and (2) what the knee does.

Read the analogy. Check the strong bridge sentence.

KITCHEN : HOUSE

____ A. A kitchen is a room in a house.

____ B. There's a kitchen in my house.

Answer A is correct. It shows a specific part-whole relationship. B is too general.

Step 3 Test the answer choices in your bridge sentence.

Read the test analogy. Then test each answer pair. Pick the pair that makes sense in your bridge sentence.

Test analogy	Bridge	Does this answer make sense?
SEE : EYE ::	You SEE with your EYE.	Yes
A. look : point	You *look* with your *point*.	No
B. walk : run	You *walk* with your *run*.	No
C. talk : mouth	You *talk* with your *mouth*.	Yes
D. nose : face	You *nose* with your *face*.	No

Answer choice C makes the most sense. The connection between SEE : EYE and TALK : MOUTH is alike. SEE and TALK are actions. An EYE and a MOUTH are used in those actions. They are both face parts, too.

TIP

Only one answer pair will make sense with a strong bridge sentence.

Read the analogy and bridge sentence. Test the answer choices in the bridge. Check the sentence that makes the best sense.

Analogy	Bridge
CLIMB : TREES ::	Kids like to CLIMB TREES.
fall : trip	A. Kids like to _____ _____.
sink : swim	B. Kids like to _____ _____.
music : sing	C. Kids like to _____ _____.
jump : rope	D. Kids like to _____ _____.

The stem pair shows an action and the thing used in that action. The only answer choice that makes sense in the bridge sentence is D. Answer A doesn't make sense. Kids don't like to fall or trip. In B, the words are opposites. In C, the word forms are in the wrong order. So, *kids like to music sing* doesn't make sense.

Some tests give you the bridge sentence. Then you pick the missing words.

Analogy sentence	Answer choices	Compares
Birds sing, while dogs—	✓ A. bark ___ B. hum ___ C. quack ___ D. run	the sounds that two animals make
Lemon is sour, while sugar is—	___ A. delicious ___ B. dry ___ C. fresh ✓ D. sweet	two opposite tastes

Check the word that best completes this analogy.

You row a canoe with a paddle in the same way you play baseball with

___ A. a bat

___ B. a diamond

___ C. home plate

___ D. a mitt

All the word choices are used in baseball, but A is the correct answer. You use a paddle to row a canoe. You use a bat to hit a ball.

Step 4 Use the process of elimination, if needed.

You may not know some words in an analogy. Then it's hard to make a strong bridge sentence. But you can use information you *do* know to make a guess. You can use the **process of elimination** to make a best guess.

To review the process of elimination, go to Chapter 1, pages 17–19.

Practice A: Read the analogies. Write bridge sentences for them.

Analogy	Bridge
LEAVES : TREE	Leaves grow on a tree.
1. SHARK : OCEAN	_____
2. SPANISH : LANGUAGE	_____
3. DAY : NIGHT	_____
4. KITCHEN : HOUSE	_____

Practice B: Solve the analogies. Use your bridge sentences from Practice A.

1. SHARK : OCEAN ::
   A. tuna : can
   B. bird : sky
   C. bear : sleep
   D. egg : chicken

2. SPANISH : LANGUAGE ::
   A. soccer : sport
   B. talking : speaking
   C. French : English
   D. checkers : chess

3. DAY : NIGHT ::
   A. morning : lunch
   B. light : vision
   C. sunlight : electricity
   D. hold : drop

4. KITCHEN : HOUSE ::
   A. classroom : school
   B. cashier : store
   C. cooking : eating
   D. door : window

Practice C: Complete the analogy sentences.

> **EXAMPLE**
>
> You beat a drum, and you hammer a—
>
> ___ A. jack   ✓ B. nail   ___ C. tool   ___ D. wood

1. Avalanches block mountain roads. Floods—

   ___ A. blow down trees   ___ C. fall on houses

   ___ B. create traffic jams   ___ D. wash away bridges

2. A car running out of gas is similar to a person—

   ___ A. getting hungry   ___ C. tripping on a rock

   ___ B. seeing a doctor   ___ D. going on vacation

SEE PAGE 176 FOR ANSWERS.

Figure Out Words in Context

Most people learn new words by hearing them **in context**. The **context** is the other words and sentences around a word. Don't stop reading as soon as you see a new word.

 ## Keys to Understanding

Strategies for Figuring Out Words in Context

1. Find nearby **synonyms** (words with similar meanings).
   Words like *small* and *little* are synonyms. *Large* and *big* are synonyms, too.

   Example: The sailor ties a knot with *deft* fingers. His hands are *trained* and *skillful*.

2. Look for **helpful punctuation**.
   Find synonyms or definitions
   - after a *dash:* —
   - after *comma + or:* **, or**
   - in *parentheses:* ( )

   Examples: a. By noon, the morning mist *evaporates—disappears*.
               b. In olden times, Egypt was ruled by a *pharaoh, or king*.
               c. Chemicals make the stream *contaminated (dirty, polluted)*.

Read the sentences. Then complete A through C below.

1. Yasmin's mother leads a scout troop. She is a *mentor*, or teacher, to many girls.

2. The Sanchez family helps the school library. This year they gave a generous *donation*—a gift of six new computers.

3. Andreus is intelligent. He is a serious thinker. He always gives *sage* answers.

4. My *colleagues* (coworkers) and I make a great team.

   Example: A *mentor* is a teacher.

   A. A *colleague* is also a _____.

   B. Another word for *donation* is _____.

   C. A *sage* person is usually _____.

The answer for A is between the parentheses: *coworker*. The answer for B is after a dash: *gift*. Synonyms for C are *intelligent* and *serious thinker*.

TIP

Many English words have *cognates* (similar words) in other languages.

For example:
magnificent
magnífico
magnifique

Cognates can also help you figure out words in context.

Keys to Understanding

Signal Words: **Figuring Out Words in Context**

Watch for words that signal a definition: *that is, such as,* or *in other words.*

EXAMPLES

A. The Hawaiian volcano, Mauna Kea, is **dormant**; *that is,* it is **sleeping, or quiet now**, but it could wake up and explode again in the future.

B. Folktales are full of **mythical** beings, *such as* **unicorns, witches,** and **elves.**

C. The fox is a **nocturnal** animal. *In other words,* it's **awake at night** and asleep during the day.

Practice: Read the paragraphs. Then complete the sentences that follow using a word from the list.

EXAMPLE

Ivan Sutherland pioneered a program called Sketchpad in 1962. That is, he made the first drawings on a large mainframe computer with a light pen.

first   last   on a computer   with a light pen

You *pioneer* an activity before others. That means you do it <u>first</u>.

1. The cabin is very secluded (with no houses nearby). You can't see it from the road. There isn't even a mailbox. We get our mail at the post office. It's a good place for peace and quiet.

    busy   friendly   plain   private

    A *secluded* place is _____.

2.

> *Dear Guests,*
>
> *You can use any food in the kitchen. There is also wood for the fireplace. But please replenish any supplies you use up. Sam at the town market will restock the food. There is extra wood in the shed.*
>
> *The Management*

finish   refill   supplies   use

The best synonym for *replenish* is _____.

3. Don't trust that man. He is unscrupulous. He tried to sell my grandfather a car. He didn't even own it! He is a liar. Don't believe anything he says!

is dishonest   is fair   sells cars   tells the truth

An *unscrupulous* salesperson probably _____.

4. Since the accident, the patient has had amnesia—he doesn't remember his name, where he lives, or why he's in El Paso. He has a driver's license. But he can't read a map.

an accidental   a driving   a memory   a musical

Amnesia is _____ problem.

5. "Lihan will persevere," says his mother. "In other words, he will keep trying. He won't give up now. He needs only five more points."

agree with his parents   finish it   get five more points   stop

Lihan *perseveres*. He doesn't _____.

6. We started this trip for fun. We never imagined such an arduous hike. The road is hard and rocky, our backpacks are heavy, and we are almost out of water.

demanding   difficult   easy   tough

Arduous is the opposite of _____.

SEE PAGE 176 FOR ANSWERS.

Strategy 18 — Analyze Compound Words and Roots, Prefixes, and Suffixes

Compound Words

A **compound word** is two small words that are put together to make a third word.

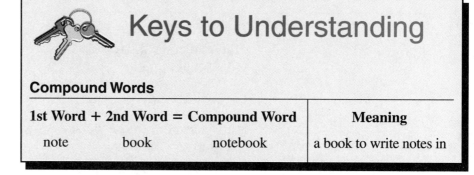

Keys to Understanding

Compound Words

1st Word + 2nd Word = Compound Word	Meaning
note book notebook	a book to write notes in

Match these compound words to their meanings. Write the correct letter.

__X__ afterthought   X. an extra idea; an idea you get later

___ 1. earthquake   A. a timepiece to wear

___ 2. firefighters   B. people who put out fires

___ 3. wristwatch   C. shaking of the earth

The word *quake* means shake, so the answer to 1 is C; 2 is B; 3 is A.

Roots, Prefixes, and Suffixes

Many words have three main parts: **roots, prefixes,** and **suffixes.**
Knowing what these word parts mean can help you understand a new word.

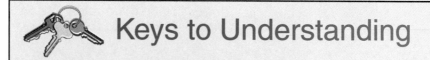

Keys to Understanding

A **root** is the *main meaning* of the word.
A **prefix** is added to the *beginning* of a word. It adds meaning to the root.
A **suffix** is added to the *end* of a word. It adds meaning to the root, too.

You can figure out new words when you know these word parts. Look at the word *microbiology.*

	Prefix	**Root**	**Suffix**
word part	*micro-*	*bio*	*-ology*
meaning	very small	life	study of

Put the meanings of the prefix, root, and suffix together. You can figure out that *microbiology* is the study of very small living things.

Here are lists of helpful word parts to learn. Add other words you know.

TIP

Sometimes word parts are also complete words.

root: *meter*
prefix: *super*
suffix: *less*

Root	**Meaning**	**Example**
annu	year	annual
aud	hear	audiotape
auto	self	automatic
biblio	book	bibliography
cent	100	percent
chron	time	chronology
cred	believe	incredible
dent	tooth	dentist
derm	skin	dermatology
dic(t)	say/speak	dictate
fract/frag	break	fraction/fragment
geo	earth	geography
gram/graph/scrip	write	telegram/graphic/script
meter	measure	thermometer
ped/pod	foot	pedal/podiatrist
phon/son	sound	telephone/sonar
psych	mind	psychology
port	carry	import
scope/spec	see	microscope/inspect
sect/seg	cut	section/segment
sphere	ball	hemisphere
syn	together	synonym
vita/vi(v)	life	vitamin/vivid

Here are some useful prefixes and suffixes to learn. Some are grouped to help you learn them more easily.

	Prefix	Meaning	Example
opposite pairs	anti-/con-/contra-	against	antiwar/contrary
	pro-	for/toward	proponent
	bene-	good, well	benefit
	mal-/mis-	bad/wrong	malady/mistake
negatives	dis-	not, opposite	disagree
	il-/im-/in-/ir-/un-	not	inactive/unhappy
numbers	demi-/hemi-/semi-	one-half	demitasse/hemisphere/semicolon
	uni-	1	unit
	bi-/di-/du-	2	bicycle/dissect/dual
	tri-	3	triplet
	quad-/quar-	4	quadruple/quarter
time or directions	circu-	around	circumference
	inter-	between	interrupt
	pre-	before	preview
	re-	again/back/bad	return
	sub-	under	subway
	trans-	across	transfer

Suffix	Meaning	Example
-en	made of	golden
-er/-ian/-ist/-or/-yst	person's work/job name	teacher/historian/typist/major/analyst
-ful/-ous	a lot of	thoughtful/joyous
-less	without	careless
-ness	state or quality of	happiness

Practice A: Match the word to its meaning. The words in *italics* are hints.

Word	Meaning
_j_ 1. chronology	a. *1/100* of a *meter*
___ 2. autobiography	b. a *book* someone writes about *his or her own life*
___ 3. anniversary	
___ 4. centimeter	c. a *broken* rule
___ 5. circumnavigate	d. carry out
___ 6. contradict	e. false *teeth*
___ 7. dentures	f. a *yearly* celebration
___ 8. infraction	g. *say the opposite of*
___ 9. subdermal	h. travel *around* the globe
___ 10. undertake	i. *under* the *skin*
	j. *time* order

Practice B: Complete the sentences with words from the box. The words in *italics* are hints about roots, prefixes, and/or suffixes.

auditorium	fearless	portable	spectators
century	✓ governor	prediction	synthesized
dictator	misunderstand	revive	

Example: He was *elected* <u>governor</u> twice. He worked hard to *lead the state*.

1. You _____. I'll *explain* again. *Then* you'll *know what I mean.*

2. She's a real _____. Everyone has to do what she *says*.

3. This plant looks *dead. But* lots of water can _____ it.

4. *One hundred* years is called a _____.

5. These ideas are *put together* very well. Your topic is well _____.

6. What *is going to happen? Tell* me *before* you read. Make a _____.

7. Bring the _____ television. It's light and *easy to carry*.

8. It's a great _____. You can *hear* and see from any seat.

9. The _____ *watched* the game in the sports arena.

10. That boy *isn't afraid*. He's _____ in the face of danger.

SEE PAGE 176 FOR ANSWERS.

Strategy 18   Analyze Compound Words and Roots, Prefixes, and Suffixes   **99**

Strategy 19

Distinguish Denotative and Connotative Meaning and Recognize Synonyms and Antonyms

Denotative and Connotative Meaning

Words can have two kinds of meaning. The **denotative** meaning is what you find in the dictionary. Denotative is also called **literal**. The **connotative** meaning is the feeling or image you get from the word. Connotative is also called **figurative**.

Read the sentences. Compare the denotative and connotative meanings of *shiver*.

	Example	Meaning
Denotative	1. The boy scouts *shiver* with cold.	shake or move
Connotative	2. The boy scouts *shiver* when they hear a ghost story.	are afraid or fearful

The denotative meaning of *shiver* is to shake or move. The connotative meaning is related to fear, a feeling.

 Keys to Understanding

Texts and Denotative and Connotative Language

- Nonfiction, newspapers, and scientific and informational texts use more denotative language.

- Fiction and poetry use more connotative language.

Read the sentences. Look at the word in *italics*. Write *D* for a denotative meaning. Write *C* for a connotative meaning.

<u>D</u> Pearls and rubies are *precious*—rare and expensive—jewels.

<u>C</u> He's so cute! What a *precious* baby!

____ 1. He hears the bad news. His face turns *pale*.

____ 2. The room is painted *pale* green.

____ 3. It is only April; but the *temperature* is over 80 degrees.

____ 4. She is so angry. She feels her *temperature* rise.

1. C He turns pale because he feels upset. Feelings are connotative.
2. D This sentence uses the dictionary meaning of *pale*—a light color.
3. D The sentence states a fact. It uses the denotative meaning of *temperature*. 4. C Anger is a feeling. Here, *temperature* has a connotative meaning.

Synonyms and Antonyms

Synonyms are words with similar meanings. Learning and using synonyms helps your vocabulary grow. Books called **thesauruses** and **synonym finders** can help. These books are like dictionaries. The words are in alphabetical order, but they have lists of synonyms instead of definitions. (You can find these online, too.)

Antonyms are words with opposite meanings. *Big* and *small* are antonyms. So are *friend–enemy, pro–con, increase–decrease*, and *love–hate*. There are many antonyms. It is helpful to learn pairs of synonyms and antonyms together. Thesauruses and synonym finders often list antonyms, too.

Make your own list of words and their synonyms and antonyms. Keep a chart like this in your notebook.

> **TIP**
> 1. Words can have more than one meaning.
> 2. Not every word has an antonym.

		Letter P
Word	Synonym	Antonym
preserve	protect, keep, save	end, destroy
pantomime	act without words, gesture	speak, do a role play
pedestrian	1. a walker 2. dull	1. a driver 2. exciting

Practice: Read this essay. Then answer the vocabulary questions below.

Multiple Intelligences

Schools often measure "intelligence" in two ways. One is verbal (good with words). The other is mathematical (good with numbers). But Dr. Howard Gardner thinks there are several kinds of intelligences and several ways to learn. One example is "musical intelligence." People who are musical learners often produce music. They appreciate it, too. They love everything about it. Students do better when teachers encourage different ways to learn. If you use a special intelligence, it strengthens. On the other hand, if you ignore a special intelligence, it weakens.

Read the boldface word. Circle the synonyms on that line. The number in parentheses (1) tells how many synonyms there are on the line. Use a dictionary or thesaurus if needed.

measure (3)	(test)	tape	(rate)	(evaluate)
1. **musical** (2)	intelligence	example	tuneful	harmonious
2. **appreciate** (1)	like	dislike	sing	weak
3. **strengthen** (3)	make stronger	make longer	fortify	reinforce
4. **weaken** (1)	make thinner	exhaust	make younger	loosen

Read the boldface word. Circle the antonym. There is only one antonym per line. Use a dictionary or thesaurus if needed.

produce	construct	form	create	(destroy)
5. **intelligence**	ability	cleverness	foolishness	brainpower
6. **ignore**	pay no attention to	notice	disregard	overlook
7. **encourage**	support	undermine	advance	hearten
8. **multiple**	several	numerous	many	single

SEE PAGE 176 FOR ANSWERS.

<table>
<tr><td></td><td>**Strategy 20**</td><td></td></tr>
</table>

Strategy 20

Identify Multiple-Meaning Words and Words Often Confused

Multiple-Meaning Words

Multiple-meaning words are words that have more than one meaning. The meaning of these words can be figured out from the context.

The word *back* has two different meanings in these pictures.

This is her *back*.

"Go *back* inside."

In picture 1, *back* means a body part. In picture 2, *back* means return.

Here are some examples of multiple-meaning words. There are many more.

Word	Meaning	Example
arms	body part guns	He holds the baby in his *arms*. The government buys *arms* for its soldiers.
bank	a place for money land along a river	I have a savings account at the *bank*. The boaters rest on the *bank* of the river.
case	a box lawsuit if	My son has a new pencil *case* for school. A lawyer wins a *case*. Mom, can you pick me up *in case* I stay for soccer?
count	matter say numbers in order	This test will *count* for 50 percent of your grade. The class is learning to *count* in Chinese.

Word	Meaning	Example
fair	nice right light festival	I like to hike on *fair* days. That judge's decisions are always *fair*. He has *fair* hair. I love to go on rides at the *fair*.
like	similar to enjoy	It's only March, but today feels *like* summer. I *like* to hike!
mean	denote not nice average	Sunshine *means* daylight. The *mean* girl pulled my hair. The math teacher asked for the *mean* of six numbers.
present	gift attending	I gave my mother a *present* on her birthday. I am *present* at school every day.
stick	attach twig	*Stick* a stamp on the letter, please. One more *stick* and the campfire will be ready.

Words Often Confused

Homonyms are words that sound alike but have different meanings and different spellings. Homonyms can be confusing. Read the whole sentence to determine the correct choice.

The words *weather* and *whether* sound the same. But *weather* means climate. *Whether* means if. Read the sentences. Are they correct?

1. The *weather* is hot today. It must be 90 degrees.

2. Ask your father *whether* you can come to my house after school.

They are both correct. Sentence 1 has two hints: *hot* and *90 degrees*. In sentence 2, you can use *if* instead of *whether* and the meaning stays the same.

Here is a list of helpful homonyms.

Homonyms	Meaning	Example
brake break	device that stops something to damage or crack time to rest	Use the hand *brake* when you park the car. *Break* the egg into a hot frying pan. I usually have a snack during my *break*.
hear here	to listen in this place	Can you *hear* the birds singing outside? Please come *here*.
its it's	belonging to it it is	The dog played with *its* ball. *It's* a red, rubber ball.
knew new	past form of *know* latest, not old	I *knew* how to multiply in fourth grade. I'm too big for my bike. I need a *new* one.
know no	to comprehend reject/negative	He *knows* how to drive. *No*. He doesn't have a car.
passed past	past form of *pass* succeeded time before now	I *passed* all the other runners! The whole class *passed* the English exam. History is the study of the *past*.
peace piece	calm, quiet/no war part, section	The war ended. The country is at *peace*. Do you want a *piece* of cake?
right write	correct opposite of left to put words on paper	Is that the *right* answer? Start marching with your *right* foot. I have to *write* a paper for history class.
their there they're	belonging to them in that place they are	This is *their* house. Sign your name *there* at the bottom. *They're* my friends from gym class.
to too two	toward also 2	Mohammed is going *to* the library. Jack is going, *too*. Jake and José are *two* boys.
way weigh	direction to measure weight	Is this the *way* to Green Street? The doctor *weighs* me at every visit.
weak week	not strong seven days	I am sick and feel *weak*. The first *week* of school is exciting.
wear where	to put on clothes in what place?	I like to *wear* my school sweater. *Where* is your next class?
who's whose	who is belonging to whom	*Who's* your math teacher this year? *Whose* book is this?
your you're	belonging to you you are	This is *your* book. You dropped it. *You're* right on time.

Other Words Often Confused

These words aren't homonyms, but they sound alike or look alike. Sometimes their meanings are very close. Learn their meanings. If you read the whole sentence to understand the context, they won't confuse you.

Words	Meaning	Example
accept except	to agree or take all but	Please *accept* this gift with our thanks. I like all my teachers *except* Mr. Howell.
affect effect	to influence result	My mood is usually *affected* by the weather. One *effect* of polluted water is sick animals.
among between	use with 3 or more use with 2	I divided the candy *among* my five friends. I can't choose *between* Mary and Alice.
than then	use in comparisons shows time sequence	History class is longer *than* band practice. First, I study. *Then*, I practice my drums.
we're were	we are past form of *are* for you, we, and they	*We're* taking a French test today. We *were* studying together.

Practice A: Read the conversations. Write the correct word on the line.

Dan: My _____*new*_____ teacher is nice.
(knew, new)

Jan: (1) _____ lucky. My teacher makes me (2) _____
(Your, You're)   (right, write)

(3) _____ pages in my notebook every (4) _____.
(to, too, two)   (weak, week)

Ben: (5) _____ running to first base?
(Who's, Whose)

Jen: I think (6) _____ Rasheed.
(it's, its)

Ben: (7) _____. Rasheed is taller (8) _____ that runner.
(Know, No)   (than, then)

Jen: That's (9) _____. Rasheed (10) _____ more, too.
(right, write)   (ways, weighs)

Ben: He's the biggest boy in school, (11) _____ for Josh.
(accept, except)

Practice B: Read the sentences. Then look at the dictionary definitions below. Write the number that matches the correct meaning.

Example: _2_ Friends are coming for dinner. Please press the tablecloth.

___ A. The government uses a special press to print money.

___ B. First, plug in the machine. Then, press the red button.

___ C. The press interviewed the movie star.

___ D. We pressed the teacher for a holiday party.

___ E. My brother knows how to press his shirts.

---

press (verb) **1.** to push down: *Press the button to ring the bell.* **2.** to iron: *I have to press my clothes for the party.* **3.** to try to influence: *The mayor pressed many people to vote for her.*—**press** (noun) **4.** a machine for printing: *Newspapers are printed on a printing press.* **5.** newspaper, television, and radio workers: *The president held a news conference with the press.*

Practice C: Read this paragraph. Cross out incorrect words. Write the correct word above each incorrect word. The first one is done for you. There are six more mistakes.

---

                                             know

    Everyone likes lollipops. But do you ~~no~~ wear the word comes from? Hear's the story about it's history: The word *lolly* was sometimes used in England too mean "tongue." The word *pop* was a peace of hard candy. Put the two words together, and you get *lollipop.* Its hard candy on a stick to lick with your tongue.

SEE PAGE 176 FOR ANSWERS.

Photocopying this page is prohibited by law.

Strategy 21

Use Content Vocabulary: Science, Social Studies, Math, and Technology

1. **Preview text features**: title, introduction, headings, maps, diagrams, captions.

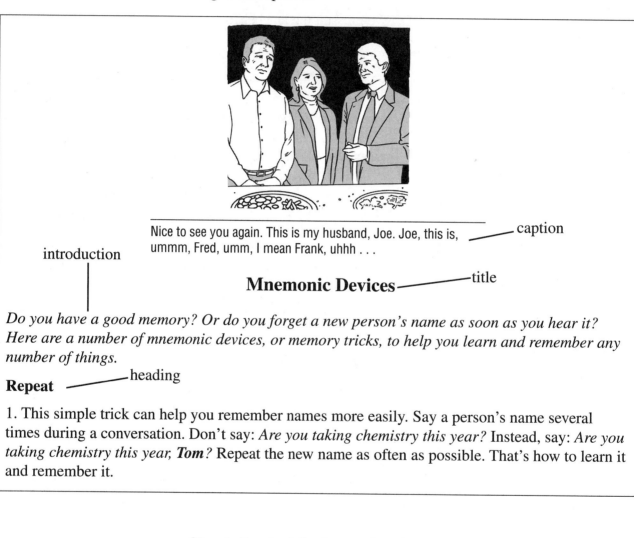

introduction

caption

Nice to see you again. This is my husband, Joe. Joe, this is, ummm, Fred, umm, I mean Frank, uhhh . . .

Mnemonic Devices ——title

Do you have a good memory? Or do you forget a new person's name as soon as you hear it? Here are a number of mnemonic devices, or memory tricks, to help you learn and remember any number of things.

Repeat —— heading

1. This simple trick can help you remember names more easily. Say a person's name several times during a conversation. Don't say: *Are you taking chemistry this year?* Instead, say: *Are you taking chemistry this year,* **Tom**? Repeat the new name as often as possible. That's how to learn it and remember it.

Check the text features that help you figure out the meaning of mnemonic devices.

___ A. picture and caption   ___ B. title   ___ C. introduction

___ D. heading   ___ E. paragraph 1

You can check any answer except B. The title *names* the subject of the reading. It doesn't explain it.

2. **Use vocabulary skills** to figure out new words in different subjects.

Look at the vocabulary in these math problems.

> Sofia and I surveyed 50 students at lunch about their favorite subjects. We recorded the data in this table.
>
> In this word problem, what does *survey* mean? (*Hint:* Use the context to figure out the meaning.)
>
> A. ask   B. teach   C. eat   D. answer

The answer is A. If you put *ask* in the sentence, the meaning is the same: *Sofia and I **asked** 50 students at lunch about their favorite subjects.*

> A square is one kind of quadrilateral. (*Hint:* Look at the prefix.)
>
> A *quadrilateral* has ——————— sides.
>
> A. 1   B. 2   C. 3   D. 4

The answer is D. The prefix *quad-* means 4. So a quadrilateral is a 4-sided figure.

> A bicycle wheel travels about 91 inches in one full turn. What is the diameter to the nearest centimeter?
>
> What is a *diameter?*
>
> A. a measurement divided into many parts
>
> B. a line that divides a figure in two parts
>
> C. the circumference of a circle
>
> D. two hundred meters

Think about the word parts of *diameter: di-* means 2 and *meter* is a measure. You can eliminate A and C. *Two* doesn't mean many parts. And a circumference is the distance around a circle. Answer D doesn't make sense. Two-hundred meters is much more than the distance a bicycle wheel turns. So the answer is B. The diameter cuts a circle into two semicircles.

Practice A: Preview the reading. Then read the passage. Complete the chart that follows.

Terra-cotta Warriors

The terra-cotta "army" at Xi'an, China

1   In 1974, farmers were digging a well in the Shaanxi province in China. They made an amazing discovery: the site of an army. The soldiers, horses, and chariots are all statues of painted terra-cotta, or hardened clay.

2   Over 7,000 figures were unearthed near the city of Xi'an, southwest of Beijing. They were buried about 2,200 years ago. No two of the life-sized statues are alike. They vary in height from about 5 1/2 to 6 1/2 feet. Each face has a different expression. Each soldier wears the uniform and carries the weapon of his rank. They wear different shoes and have individual hairstyles. Even each horse is unique.

3   Archaeologists found the warriors lined up. They look ready to march into war. This model army was made to protect an emperor's tomb for eternity. An emperor ordered a replica of his real army.

Write synonyms and/or antonyms for each word.

	Synonyms	Antonyms
warrior	soldier	
1. terra-cotta		
2. unearthed		
3. unique		
4. replica		

Practice B: Look at the map. Read the caption. Write the correct word on the line.

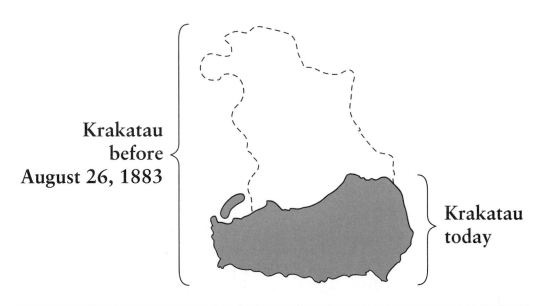

Krakatau
before
August 26, 1883

Krakatau
today

Karato, Idonesia: On August 26, 1883, the volcano on Krakatau Island erupted. It was a catastrophe—one of the worst natural disasters ever. It destroyed most of the island. Today, Krakatau is a fraction of its original size. Ash blocked the sun completely for two and a half days. Winds transported the ash as far as New York City. The explosion created *tsunamis* (waves) 120 feet high. Scientists predict it will erupt again in the future. But they think the island is safe for the next few hundred years.

Example: (disaster, volcano) Another word for *catastrophe* is
disaster.

1. (bigger, smaller) *Today, Krakatau is a fraction of its original size*. This means the island is _____ than it used to be.

2. (carried, removed) *Winds transported the ash as far as New York City* means winds _____ the ash.

3. (ash, water) *Tsunamis* are made of _____ .

Photocopying this page is prohibited by law.

Practice C: Read the directions for programming a cell phone. Then complete the sentences.

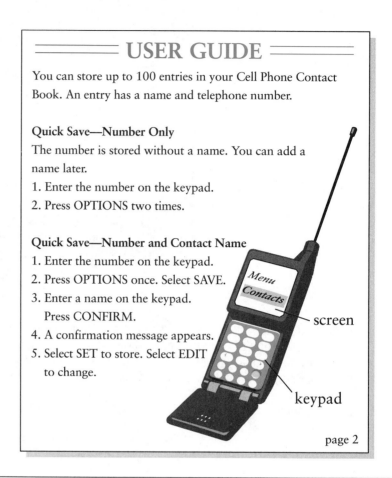

===== **USER GUIDE** =====

You can store up to 100 entries in your Cell Phone Contact Book. An entry has a name and telephone number.

Quick Save—Number Only
The number is stored without a name. You can add a name later.
1. Enter the number on the keypad.
2. Press OPTIONS two times.

Quick Save—Number and Contact Name
1. Enter the number on the keypad.
2. Press OPTIONS once. Select SAVE.
3. Enter a name on the keypad.
   Press CONFIRM.
4. A confirmation message appears.
5. Select SET to store. Select EDIT to change.

screen

keypad

page 2

| a confirmation | ✓ a contact | an edit | an entry |

Example: Meg Freeman is *a contact.*

1. A name stored with a number is _____.

2. The message saying that the information is correct is _____.

3. Make _____ to change information.

SEE PAGE 177 FOR ANSWERS.

Mark your answers on the Answer Grid.

Read this article. Then answer Questions 1 through 10.

Robots

1   For years, the only robots around were the stars of space movies. Nowadays, robots are everywhere in everyday life. They assemble cars and trucks. They drive trains. They go into hard-to-reach places like pipes and make repairs. They help doctors perform difficult operations. They even clean houses, explore the bottom of the sea, and roam the surface of Mars.

2   For many centuries people dreamed of making machines that acted like humans. In 1495, the great artist and scientist Leonardo da Vinci drew plans for a mechanical man. In the 1950s and 1960s, advances in electronics and computers made real robots possible. Every robot runs a computer program. Programs are sets of instructions. They tell the robot what to do. Sensors in some robots help them "feel" their surroundings. Then they take that information and perform the actions they were built for.

3   Robots are perfect for jobs that need exact, repetitive movements. Can you do the same thing ten thousand times a day, never take a break, and never make a mistake? A robot can. Human workers get bored doing the same thing over and over. Robots don't get bored. They can do the same task in the same way over and over. And when a battery runs down, recharging it is easy.

4   Other robots are designed to do dangerous work. They work where the air is toxic. They go where it's too hot or cold for humans. They move bombs away from people and blow the bombs up safely.

5   Medical robots let surgeons perform delicate procedures too difficult for human hands. These robots can move precisely to the right place and in the right way. Surgeons also use them to perform remote operations. Patients are in other places, sometimes hundreds, or even thousands of miles away.

6   Robot landers have traveled to Mars. They used their observation sensors to scan the ground for a safe place to land. They rolled across the planet's surface on special wheels. They gathered information about soil and rocks. They took pictures and transmitted them back to Earth.

(Continued on next page)

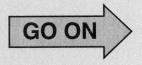

7   Today, robots even help around the house. You can buy a small, round robot vacuum cleaner that cleans a room by itself. When the device bumps into a wall, it turns and moves the other way. When it hits obstacles, like chairs, it goes around them. Its sensors know when it's no longer picking up dirt. The information tells the robot the floor is clean. That's when the robot stops.

8   Will robots ever be as smart as people? Will they be creative? Will they think on their own? Some scientists believe it will happen some day. But most think that robots will always be machines that must be told what to do. What do you think? Can you imagine a time when your best friend is a robot?

---

1 Which definition represents the meaning of the word *star* as used in paragraph 1 of the reading?

   A. 5-pointed shape

   B. a sun

   C. famous person

   D. sparkling light in the night sky

2 Solve this analogy.

   surgeon : operates :: machinist : ____

   A. assembles

   B. explores

   C. performs

   D. scans

3 Here are four definitions of the word *program* as they appear in the dictionary. Which definition matches the word's use in the reading passage?

   A. a list of events in a public presentation

   B. a scheduled radio or television show

   C. a course of study in school

   D. computer commands

4 Which word in the passage comes from the Latin root meaning 100?

   A. artist

   B. centuries

   C. mechanical

   D. scientist

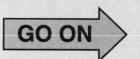

5 Read this sentence from the passage:

> Other robots are designed to do dangerous work. They work where the air is *toxic*.

In this sentence, what does *toxic* mean?

A. beneficial

B. deadly

C. healthful

D. vigorous

6 In paragraph 5, what does the word *remote* mean?

A. clicker

B. close

C. faraway

D. small chance

7
> They used their observation sensors to *scan* the ground for a safe place to land.

In this sentence, what does *scan* mean?

A. look

B. drive

C. dig

D. fly over

8 In paragraph 6, the word *transmit* means—

A. collect

B. look at

C. send

D. stop

9 What does the word *device* mean in the following sentence?

> When the *device* bumps into a wall, it turns and moves the other way.

A. helper

B. machine

C. plan

D. sensor

10 Read the following sentence.

> When it hits *obstacles,* like chairs, it goes around them.

An *obstacle* probably—

A. changes direction

B. cleans a room

C. gets in the way

D. is something to sit on

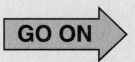

GO ON

Photocopying this page is promoted by law.

Endangered Cheetahs

1   The cheetah is a large cat with spots like a leopard. It is a fierce hunter and the fastest animal on earth. Cheetahs have two main habitats—grasslands and deserts in Africa and Asia. African cheetahs are abundant. They have enough space and food to survive in large numbers. But Asiatic cheetahs are an endangered species. According to one scientist, there are only a few hundred left in the world. The last Asiatic cheetah in captivity was 9-year-old Marita. She was found as a cub and raised by zookeepers.

2   The biggest enemy to the Asiatic cheetah's survival is its human predators. Poachers sneak into protected areas to catch them. Their speeding cars run over the cats. Poachers also hunt gazelles, foxes, and hares—the cheetah's primary food. (Some gazelles are as rare as cheetahs.) Farmers kill the big cats when they invade farms looking for food.

3   Iran is the country with the most Asiatic cheetahs. The animals are safe in a large wildlife refuge supported by the Iranian government. But cheetahs avoid people, so they are very hard to spot even there. Scientists know when a cheetah is in an area by its tracks. Those large paw prints are all most researchers ever see of a cheetah. But scientists are elated anyway. They hope to see more and more tracks as the cheetah population in the refuge grows.

11 In paragraph 1, what does the word *habitats* mean?

A. deserts

B. clothing

C. routines

D. territories

12 Read the following passage.

> African cheetahs are abundant. They have enough space and food to survive in large numbers.

An abundant number of cheetahs probably means they are—

A. plentiful

B. rare

C. inadequate

D. overflowing

13 Which words from the passage have nearly OPPOSITE meanings?

A. Africa, Asia

B. endangered, safe

C. gazelles, hares

D. scientists, researchers

14 In paragraph 1, what does the word *zookeeper* mean?

A. helper

B. janitor

C. caretaker

D. warden

15

> The biggest enemy to the Asiatic cheetah's survival is its human *predators*.

In this sentence, what does *predators* mean?

A. cars

B. hunters

C. researchers

D. scientists

16 In paragraph 2, what does the word *poachers* mean?

A. egg cookers

B. racers

C. robbers

D. townspeople

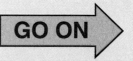

GO ON

17 What does the word *refuge* mean in the following sentence?

> **The animals are safe in a large wildlife refuge supported by the Iranian government.**

A. immigrant

B. protected place

C. say no

D. waste

18 Here are four definitions of the word *track* as they appear in the dictionary. Which definition matches the word's use in the reading passage?

A. mark left by something that has passed

B. a path for a train to move along

C. a sports activity

D. to follow

STOP. THIS IS THE END OF THE REVIEW TEST.
SEE PAGE 178 FOR ANSWERS AND EXPLANATIONS.

Chapter 6

Put It All Together

Learn to Read a Passage Fast and Carefully

Good test takers **do not know every word** on a reading test. They **do know how to read** a passage fast and carefully.

In this section, you will learn how to be a good test taker. You will learn how to work fast and carefully with a reading passage.

What to Expect

A reading passage can be short or long. Some passages are three or four paragraphs. Others are longer than a page. Two passages can be read together. Questions about the passage follow the order of the reading. You can usually find:

- answers to the **first questions** at the **beginning** of the reading
- answers to the **middle questions** in the **middle** of the reading
- answers to the **last questions** at the **end** of the reading

The reading passages will be new to you. You will find new vocabulary and new ideas in them. But all the information you need to answer the questions is in the reading passages.

Check the *true* statement about taking reading tests.

_____ A. Good test takers know every word in a reading passage.

_____ B. All reading passages are four paragraphs long.

_____ C. The answer to the first question is at the end of a passage.

_____ D. Reading passages on the reading test are in your textbooks.

_____ E. Good test takers work fast and carefully with new material.

Only E is true. You don't need to know every word. Reading passages on tests can be long or short. Questions follow the test in sequence. Reading passages are all new.

What to Do *Before* You Read a Passage

1. Read the directions.

They tell you exactly what to do and what not to do.

> Read "The River That Stopped." Then answer Questions 22 through 26.

2. Read any prologue or introduction.

It may have important background information.

> **My Ántonia**
> This novel is set in a remote area of Nebraska in the late 19th century. It is the story of native-born and immigrant families learning to cope with the beauty and bleakness of frontier life.

3. Look at pictures, charts, maps, graphs, captions, or headings.

They will help you understand the passage better.

> Supporting details help you understand the main idea.

What to Do As You Read a Passage

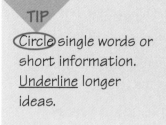

TIP

Circle single words or short information. Underline longer ideas.

You already know a lot about reading tests. You worked hard for the skills you need. In this section, you will learn how to use those skills to find answers.

Look for information *as you read* a passage. Circle or underline information as you read. Then you can find it again fast.

As you read, mark:

- words you don't know

- important ideas and details (dates, numbers, facts, details, etc.)

- literary forms (simile, metaphor, repetition, rhyme, etc.)

- problem resolution

1. Circle words you don't know.

Test questions may ask about words you don't know. Circle new words as you read so you will be able to find them again quickly. Then use your reading skills to figure out their meaning.

Ancient Egyptian pharaohs began their education before they were five. These kings-in-training studied hieroglyphics and mathematics. They practiced their writing and math exercises on papyrus, which was made from the sedge plant found on the banks of the Nile.

The words *pharaohs* and *hieroglyphics* are important. They may be new, too. So circle them as you read. Then you can find them quickly. You can look for context hints nearby to help you figure out the meaning. Underline important information, too.

Complete this analogy.
count : mathematics :: _____ : hieroglyphics

A. study   B. write   C. practice   D. find

Information in the third sentence gives the correct answer, B, *write*. The word *pharaoh* is also circled. But there is no question about it. That's okay. You won't be asked about everything you circle or underline. Circle or underline all the important parts of the passage as you read. That will give you more time later to think about your answers.

Read and circle words you don't know.

Black bears eat hundreds of pounds of roots, nuts, and berries each year. They roam over huge tracts of land to forage for the food they need. These vegetarians can starve if their territory is too small.

The word that means *to hunt or search* is _____.

The correct answer is *forage*. Did you circle it as you read?

2. Take notes as you read. Look at this sample reading passage.

The River That Stopped	My Notes
1 The Rio Grande is the <u>second longest river</u> in the United States. It is almost <u>2,000 miles long</u>. It flows from the mountains of Colorado to the Gulf of Mexico. The river forms part of the border between the United States and Mexico. In Mexico, they call the river by another name: (Rio Bravo).	important details
2 One morning, a woman called the local newspaper. "You'd better come down to the Rio Grande," she said. "<u>Our friend</u> is shorter than he used to be!"	personification: friend = river
3 (Although) the editor was (skeptical), he sent a reporter to see what the woman was talking about. The reporter was amazed to see that the river *was* shorter. It had suddenly stopped 300 feet from the Gulf of Mexico because a (sandbar) was in the way. Only a trickle of water was dribbling through to the gulf.	contrast/new word compound word
4 Sand gets (churned) up from the river bottom as water runs downstream. For centuries, the strong <u>current</u> pushed the sand downstream as the river flowed. Now, however, the Rio Grande is so (shallow) and slow near its <u>mouth</u> that the current is too weak to push the sand out of the way.	new word new word/multiple-meaning words
5 Many people walk along the Rio Grande every day. They love the river, and they don't want to walk along a sandbar. After the newspaper published the story of the river that stopped, <u>some engineers arrived to push the sand away with a bulldozer</u>. Then the Rio Grande flowed into the Gulf of Mexico again, and people could walk along the river they loved once more.	resolution

3. Answer the questions.

Easy questions Do all the easy questions first. If a question is too hard, go on to the next one. When you finish all the questions you can answer fast, try the hard ones again.

Hard questions Use the process of elimination.[1] It can help your chances of getting a correct answer.

What to Do If You Are Out of Time

Sometimes the test ends before you finish all the questions. Don't leave any blanks on your answer sheet. *Always make a guess.* To get the best possible score, pick one letter, and mark *all your blank answers with the same letter.* You will have a better chance of getting some right.

Jan and Nan don't finish the last seven questions, so they guess. Here is part of their answer grids. The answers in blue are correct.

Jan's answer	Nan's answer
44. Ⓐ Ⓑ Ⓒ Ⓓ	44. Ⓐ Ⓑ Ⓒ Ⓓ
45. Ⓐ Ⓑ Ⓒ Ⓓ	45. Ⓐ Ⓑ Ⓒ Ⓓ
46. Ⓐ Ⓑ Ⓒ Ⓓ	46. Ⓐ Ⓑ Ⓒ Ⓓ
47. Ⓐ Ⓑ Ⓒ Ⓓ	47. Ⓐ Ⓑ Ⓒ Ⓓ
48. Ⓐ Ⓑ Ⓒ Ⓓ	48. Ⓐ Ⓑ Ⓒ Ⓓ
49. Ⓐ Ⓑ Ⓒ Ⓓ	49. Ⓐ Ⓑ Ⓒ Ⓓ
50. Ⓐ Ⓑ Ⓒ Ⓓ	50. Ⓐ Ⓑ Ⓒ Ⓓ

Jan picks different letters for each answer. She gets one answer right. Nan uses the same letter for all her answers. She gets two answers right.

Using one letter for all blank answers can give you a better score.

---

[1]Review Chapter 1, pages 17–19, for the process of elimination.

Mark your answer on the Answer Grid.

1. This excerpt is BEST described as nonfiction rather than fiction because it—

   A. didn't really happen
   B. includes surprising details
   C. makes guesses about the future
   D. provides factual information

2. In paragraph 2, the author writes, "Our friend is shorter than he used to be!" This sentence has an example of—

   A. a simile
   B. a flashback
   C. personification
   D. setting

> Although the editor was *skeptical*, he sent a reporter to see what the woman was talking about.

3. In this sentence from the story, *skeptical* means that the editor—

   A. is the boss
   B. completely believes the woman
   C. isn't convinced the story was true
   D. is also a reporter

4. In paragraph 4, the author writes, "For centuries, the strong current pushed the sand downstream as the river flowed." What does *current* mean in this sentence?

   A. moving water
   B. electricity
   C. fashion
   D. power

5. The sandbar formed at the mouth of the Rio Grande because—

   A. water flowed for centuries
   B. the river was shallow and slow there
   C. the current was very fast
   D. engineers used a bulldozer

Answer Grid

1. Ⓐ Ⓑ Ⓒ **Ⓓ**

2. Ⓐ Ⓑ Ⓒ Ⓓ

3. Ⓐ Ⓑ Ⓒ Ⓓ

4. Ⓐ Ⓑ Ⓒ Ⓓ

5. Ⓐ Ⓑ Ⓒ Ⓓ

Answer Key and Explanations

1. A. Incorrect. This event *did* happen.
   B. Incorrect. *Surprising details* can be real (nonfiction) or made up (fiction).
   C. Incorrect. There is no information in the reading about predictions.
   D. Correct. Nonfiction means *based on facts*.

2. A. Incorrect. A simile is a comparison with *like* or *as*.
   B. Incorrect. Flashback is a literary device that interrupts the present with a scene or memory from the past.
   C. Correct. Personification describes animals or things (like the river) by giving them human qualities (our friend).
   D. Incorrect. Setting refers to *place*. This sentence describes a *thing*.

3. A. Incorrect. **Tricky Answer:** It's true that the editor is the boss of the reporter. But *skeptical* describes how the editor *thinks and feels*, not what he *does*.
   B. Incorrect. The word *Although* sets up a contrast, showing that *skeptical* means the opposite of *believed*.
   C. Correct. *Although* sets up a contrast between what the editor does (sends a reporter) and how the editor feels (skeptical). So *skeptical* means the editor has a hard time believing the river is shorter.
   D. Incorrect. The editor is the boss—because he tells the reporter where to go and what to do.

4. A. Correct. From the phrase *as the river flowed* you can tell that current has to do with moving water.
   B. Incorrect. There is nothing in the reading about electricity.
   C. Incorrect. There is nothing in the reading about current fashions.
   D. Incorrect. There is nothing in the reading about power.

5. A. Incorrect. The signal word in question 5 is *because*. This is a detail that doesn't give a cause for the sandbar.
   B. Correct. The signal word is *because*. Look for a *cause* for the sandbar (effect).
   C. Incorrect. Fast currents are strong. They keep sand moving, so they don't create sandbars.
   D. Incorrect. The engineers used a bulldozer to remove the sandbar, not to make it.

Now use your skills to put it all together on Cumulative Practice Test 1.

Cumulative Practice Test 1

Mark your answers on the Answer Grid.

Read this article. Look at the Schedule of Highlights. Then answer Questions 1 through 9.

Polar Bear Jump Off	**My Notes**

Polar Bear Jump Off

1   It started as a one-day event in Seward, Alaska, in 1986. A few brave individuals promised to jump into icy Resurrection Bay to raise money for charity. The jumpers jumped. The money was raised. And a great new tradition began.

2   Today the Polar Bear Jump Off is a statewide festival. It attracts thousands of visitors each year. It's now three days long with lots of activities for the whole family. There's a dogsled race, children's games, cross-country skiing, bowling on ice, and an arts-and-crafts fair. You can buy a date at a fund-raising auction, see fireworks, watch street parades, and join a slippery salmon toss. (Competitors pair up and toss a slimy salmon to each other. Each time they throw the salmon, they move back a foot. The more a fish is tossed, the slimier it gets.)

3   But the highlight of the festival is still the "Plunge" into Resurrection Bay on the third Saturday in January. More than 100 Polar Bears, or jumpers, who are normal folks the rest of the year, get to act crazy. Many jumpers dress in costumes for the big parade to the harbor. You can see King Neptune, the Roman god of the sea, a ballet dancer, or a bug. Polar Bears even have their own official song.

4   At 12:30, the swimmers jump in and swim as long as they can. Before Brenda Lane took the Plunge, she thought the water wouldn't be too cold. Afterward, she admitted that her legs were so numb, "my toes were ice cubes!"

5   "Sometimes the Plunge takes place in a snowstorm," one of the festival's organizers said. "Snowstorms are good. People don't like it when the weather is too warm."

(Continued on next page)

GO ON

6   When the swimmers climb out of the water, they're handed a blanket to put around their shoulders. They walk as fast as they can to a nearby building where they can dry off, get dressed, and warm up. People cheer them all the way there.

7   The good-natured Polar Bears are generous and willing to do almost anything for a good cause. But they don't want to be cold *all the time*. That's why the top Polar Bear prize, the Nanook, is a pair of airline tickets to Hawaii.

My Notes

Schedule of Highlights

Friday

9:00 a.m.–noon	Dogsled races.
11:00 a.m.–4:00 p.m.	Cross-country skiing contests.
6:00 p.m.–10:00 p.m.	Steak Night — Live music, American Legion Hall.
7:00 p.m.–9:30 p.m.	Date Auction, Seward Elks Club. All proceeds go to charity.
10:00 p.m.	Fireworks over Seward Boat Harbor.

Saturday

8:00 a.m.–11:00 a.m.	An Alaskan breakfast, Town Hall. Bring the family.
11:30 a.m.–noon	Polar Bear Costume Parade. Downtown to Seward Boat Harbor.
12:30 p.m.	Polar Bear Plunge, Seward Boat Harbor.
2:00 p.m.–4:00 p.m.	Children's Winter Carnival, AVTIC Gym.
2:00 p.m.–4:00 p.m.	Slippery Salmon Toss. Entry fee for charity: $5.
3:30 p.m.–4:30 p.m.	Bed-Making Contest. Entry fee for charity: $2.
5:45 p.m.	Polar Bear Plunge Awards.
7:00 p.m.	Lip-Sync Contest at the Seward Resort. Entry fee for charity: $5.
7:00 p.m.	Oyster-Slurping Contest, Seward Fish House.
8:30 p.m.	Polar Bear Karaoke Contest. Entry fee for charity: $5.

Sunday

11:00 a.m.–3:00 p.m.	Hot dogs, baked potatoes, chili . . . yum! Seward Resort.
11:00 a.m.–2:00 p.m.	Furry Flurry Dog Show. Enter your dog for charity: $2.
11:00 a.m.–2:00 p.m.	Goofy Golf, Polar Bowling, and Snowman Contest.
1:00 p.m.–3:00 p.m.	Locks of Love—haircuts for charity: $10 per head/$25 per family.

GO ON →

1 All of the following tell the reader about the setting of the Polar Bear Jump Off, EXCEPT—

A   in Seward, Alaska, in 1986

B   into icy Resurrection Bay

C   on the third Saturday in January

D   more than 100 Polar Bears

2 Which statement is a fact?

A   Sometimes the plunge takes place in a snowstorm.

B   Snowstorms are good.

C   People don't like it when the weather is too warm.

D   Her toes were ice cubes.

3 Finish this analogy with a word from the reading.

Jumpers plunge into the bay, just as _____ toss a fish in the air.

A   competitors

B   fund-raisers

C   organizers

D   bowlers

4 Which two words are the closest in meaning?

A   charity, awards

B   festival, carnival

C   normal, crazy

D   skiing, golf

5 **Which item is described in both the reading and the schedule?**

A   Bed-Making Contest

B   Slippery Salmon Toss

C   Arts-and-Crafts Fair

D   the Nanook

6 **The purpose of the Schedule of Highlights is to—**

A   inform

B   entertain

C   persuade

D   influence

7 **Where can you have an Alaskan breakfast?**

A   American Legion Hall

B   Seward Boat Harbor

C   Seward Resort

D   Town Hall

8 **Look at this diagram of information from the Schedule of Highlights.**

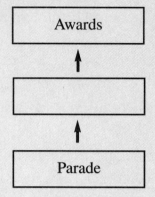

Which event belongs in the empty box?

A   Breakfast

B   Plunge

C   Bed Making

D   Oyster Slurping

9 **A family watches the Polar Bear Parade and Plunge, enters the Slippery Salmon Toss, puts their dog in the Furry Flurry Dog Show, and gets haircuts for all three children. How much money do they pay?**

A $30

B $32

C $35

D $37

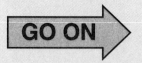

The Everglades	**My Notes**

1   Much of the Everglades in southern Florida looks like an open prairie. However, don't be fooled. Most of this low, flat plain is really a vast, shallow river that moves very, very slowly. The water is hidden below reeds and tall, grasslike plants called sawgrass. Sawgrass got its name because its leaves have tiny sharp "teeth" along the edges. The sawgrass grows everywhere, even during the winter dry season. That's why the Everglades is known as the "River of Grass."

2   The Everglades has many different ecosystems, from swamps to dense woods. Small changes in the elevation of the land can create very different communities of plants and animals. All it takes is for the land to be a few inches higher or lower. The same is true for differences in the salinity, or salt level, of the water. Changes occur when salt water from the surrounding bay mixes with the fresh water of the Everglades. Seasonal changes also make a big difference. The summer months are rainy. The winter months are dry.

3   Tangled forests of mangrove trees are full of vitality in the coastal channels and winding rivers around the tip of south Florida. Red mangroves have roots like stilts that boost the trees above the water. Many different species of birds live in the mangrove forests. They like to nest there because they can find their favorite meals of shrimp and fish in the water below.

4   There are cypress trees that can survive in several feet of water. There are also dense woods on land that is only a few inches above the water. Stunted cypress trees grow in the poorest soil on drier land.

5   The Everglades is the largest remaining subtropical wilderness in the United States. Thousands of species of plants, birds, animals, fish, and reptiles make their home here. It is the only place in the world where alligators and crocodiles live side by side. But today, more than half the area of the original Everglades no longer exists. Large areas were drained and filled in over many years. Farms and houses replaced wetlands.

(Continued on next page)

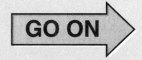

6 | Many species of wildlife are threatened or endangered. Billions of dollars are now being spent to repair the damage. The government and many other groups are involved in the effort. It's the biggest, most complicated project of its kind ever attempted. | **My Notes**

10 The Everglades looks like solid ground even though it—

A   is a river

B   has sawgrass

C   is in Florida

D   is dry in winter

11 What does the word *ecosystems* mean in this passage?

> The Everglades has many different *ecosystems*, from swamps to dense woods. Small changes in the elevation of the land can create very different communities of plants and animals.

A   environments

B   forests

C   marshes

D   organizations

12 In paragraph 2, what does *salinity* mean?

A   height

B   rainfall

C   salt level

D   season

13 Which of the following can cause changes in the ecosystems in the Everglades?

A   dry winters

B   red mangrove roots

C   stunted cypress

D   bird species

Strategies for Test Taking Success: Reading © Thomson Heinle

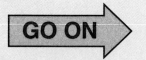

14 **Which sentence from the reading best summarizes paragraph 3?**

  A *Tangled forests of mangrove trees are full of vitality in the coastal channels and winding rivers around the tip of south Florida.*

  B *Red mangroves have roots like stilts that boost the trees above the water.*

  C *Many different species of birds live in the mangrove forests.*

  D *They like to nest there because they can find their favorite meals of shrimp and fish in the water below.*

15 **What was the effect of draining and filling the wetlands of the Everglades?**

  A Crocodiles and alligators live side by side.

  B It is the last wilderness in the United States.

  C Much of the original Everglades has disappeared.

  D Vacationers don't fish there.

16 **Which word from the passage comes from the Latin root meaning "life"?**

  A prairie

  B mangrove

  C vitality

  D subtropical

17 **The information in the article could best be used for a student research project on—**

  A damage to the American wilderness

  B ecosystems in the Everglades

  C tourism in southern Florida

  D trees of the Everglades

Photocopying this page is prohibited by law.

OUT MORNING	My Notes
by Emily Dickinson	

1   Will there really be a morning?
2   Is there such a thing as day?
3   Could I see it from the mountains
4   If I were as tall as they?

5   Has it feet like water-lilies?
6   Has it feathers like a bird?
7   Is it brought from famous countries
8   Of which I have never heard?

9   Oh, some scholar! Oh, some sailor!
10   Oh, some wise man from the skies!
11   Please to tell a little pilgrim
12   Where the place called morning lies!

18   **All these lines from the poem use similes EXCEPT—**

    A   *Could I see it from the mountains If I were as tall as they?*

    B   *Has it feet like water-lilies?*

    C   *Has it feathers like a bird?*

    D   *Is it brought from famous countries Of which I have never heard?*

19   **What is the theme of this poem?**

    A   Nature is full of mystery.

    B   People never know when they will see their last morning.

    C   People don't know when the sun will rise.

    D   Pilgrims have to ask different people for directions.

20   **This poem is written—**

    A   from a first-person point of view

    B   as a flashback

    C   to describe a character

    D   all of the above

21   **Which of the following BEST describes the poet's mood?**

    A   angry

    B   cheerful

    C   wondering

    D   pleased

22   **In line 11, *pilgrim* refers to the—**

    A   poet

    B   sailor

    C   scholar

    D   wise man

GO ON

Strategies for Test Taking Success: Reading © Thomson Heinle

Northeast Stadium

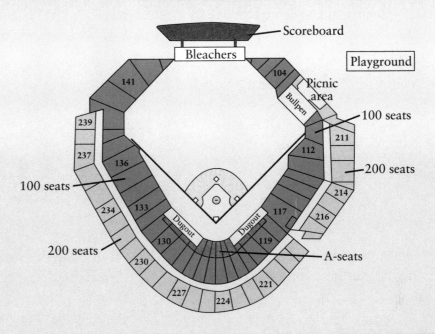

Northeast Stadium

Background This is Northeast Stadium, where the Eagles play baseball. Five years ago, the team's old stadium was torn down. It was a relic of an earlier era. It was falling apart. The seats were uncomfortable. There were many seats with obstructed views, making it hard to see what was happening on the field. The food was pretty bad. Attendance was down. Fewer people came every year. Families spent their money doing other things, like going to amusement parks.

New Seating The A-seats are the ones closest to home plate and the dugouts where the players sit. They are on the same level as the field. Servers bring food and drinks to people who sit in the A-seats. These are the most expensive seats in the stadium. All the other seats at ground level begin with the number 1, for first level. They are divided into sections. Sections get less expensive as they get farther and farther from home plate. There are more seats on the second level of the stadium. These sections begin with the number 2. The seats above the baseball diamond are more expensive than the ones that extend toward right and left fields. Seats in the bleachers are the farthest away and the cheapest. Because there is no roof above them, they can get very hot in the sun.

(Continued on next page)

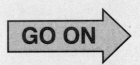

Photocopying this page is prohibited by law.

New Services The new stadium has everything the old one didn't. The seats are comfortable. The views are excellent. Snack bars serve not only hot dogs and ice cream, but also special sandwiches and salads. Families love coming here. There's a picnic area behind the bullpen. Families can picnic and watch the game until they're finished eating. Then they go back to their regular seats. Behind the picnic area there's a playground for young children and a place to practice hitting a baseball.

There's an electronic scoreboard that gives all sorts of information about the game and the players. It shows close-ups of important plays, just like a giant television. When an Eagles player hits a home run, the scoreboard displays electronic fireworks. Northeast Stadium is considered one of the best parks in the country. Let the Eagles fly!

23 The Eagles knew fans weren't happy with the old stadium because—

A attendance was down

B seats were more expensive

C the scoreboard was too plain

D the snack bars only sold special sandwiches and salads

24 Which sentence best states the main idea of the section "New Seating"?

A The new Northeast Stadium has four kinds of seats.

B The seats at ground level all cost about the same amount.

C The bleachers are cheap, but far away.

D Fans like to sit near the dugouts so they can see the players.

25 Complete this analogy with a word from the reading.
One view was clear and visible, but another was blocked and—

A displayed

B obstructed

C spent

D torn down

26 What can you conclude from the information about Northeast Stadium provided in this reading selection and seating chart?

A The best seats are opposite the bullpen.

B It's hardest to see the scoreboard from the bleachers.

C Fans have to leave the stadium to have a picnic.

D People in the A-seats are the best fans.

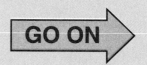

GO ON

Strategies for Test Taking Success: Reading © Thomson Unida

27

> They are on the same *level* as the field.

What does *level* mean in this sentence?

A aim

B height

C equal

D knock down

28 Instead of going to amusement parks, children at the new Northeast Stadium can—

A play in the baseball diamond between innings

B see fireworks in the sky

C hit baseballs

D watch their favorite players on a giant television

29 Which of the following statements from the reading is a fact?

A The food was pretty bad.

B Families love coming here.

C Servers bring food and drinks to people who sit in the A-seats.

D Northeast Stadium is considered one of the best parks in the country.

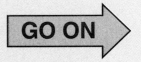

GO ON

Photocopying this page is prohibited by law.

Read this story. Then answer Questions 30 through 42.

Golden Dreams[2]	**My Notes**

1   In the 1700s, New York City was a small place. Wolfert Webber lived on a farm outside of town. He grew cabbages that were famous for being the best for miles around. The city was growing bigger and more prosperous, and Wolfert saw wealthy people everywhere he looked. It made him jealous. Why couldn't he be rich instead of just a cabbage farmer?

2   He and his wife had a daughter named Amy. Amy admired a young man named Dirk very much. Dirk was poor. Wolfert wanted his daughter to marry a rich man. So he discouraged her from seeing Dirk.

3   Wolfert Webber was so determined to become rich, he listened carefully to any stories about buried treasure. One of Wolfert's neighbors said that a group of men had recently been seen digging nearby. They were searching for a pot of gold buried in an orchard.

4   An old Dutch governor once owned the orchard. He buried the gold on a night when the moon was full. But he died before he could return to the spot.

5   One day Wolfert saw a stranger at the local inn. The stranger had a terrible scar down his face. He looked like a pirate. Maybe he knew where the buried treasure was. Maybe he was there to get it.

6   For three nights, Wolfert went to sleep and dreamed of a huge treasure buried on his farm. When he told his friends, they all said, "A dream repeated three times always turns out to be true." So he went out to dig in his fields. He dug every night by the light of a lantern. Soon his cabbage fields were ruined. "You're digging up all the cabbages!" his wife complained. But he told her not to worry. "Soon we'll be rich!" he promised.

7   All summer and fall he dug for treasure. Wolfert didn't have his usual crop of cabbages to sell, and he had to spend his savings. His neighbors thought he was crazy. The only person who still visited the family was Dirk. He still loved Amy, even though she was now poor.

8   Months later, Wolfert heard that pirates buried something along the river. No one believed the story except Wolfert. He

[2] Adapted from Washington Irving, "Golden Dreams."

GO ON ▷

decided to find the place. He climbed up a steep hill along the river and found a boulder marked with three crosses. Was this the place? He dug for hours. Finally, his shovel hit something hard. Was it a chest of gold?

9   Suddenly, Wolfert heard a noise. The stranger with the scarred face looked down at him. Wolfert dropped his shovel and ran. A hand grabbed Wolfert by the sleeve. Then another hand grabbed his other sleeve. Was this another pirate?

10   Wolfert pulled away. But just then he lost his footing. He began to slide down the steep hill toward the water. He bounced from rock to rock and bush to bush.

11   Wolfert woke up later, on the ground. He was surprised to see Dirk. Dirk explained that Wolfert's wife begged Dirk to follow Wolfert. It was Dirk who grabbed Wolfert to keep the stranger from hurting him. No one ever learned if Wolfert really found a chest of gold. Dirk went back later, but he found nothing there.

12   Wolfert was badly hurt. He called in a lawyer to write his will. Weakly, Wolfert told the lawyer that he wanted his farm to go to his family, including Dirk, who would soon marry Amy.

13   "Do you mean the land where the town plans to build a big road?" asked the lawyer. "Whoever inherits that land will be very rich."

14   "Rich?" asked Wolfert. He sat up in bed. "Very rich?"

15   "Yes," said the lawyer. "People want land on both sides of the road to build new houses and shops."

16   Wolfert felt better right away. Soon he felt good enough to get out of bed and make plans for the rest of his farm. His neighbors said that Wolfert now grew money instead of cabbages. Wolfert's golden dreams finally came true.

Photocopying this page is prohibited by law.

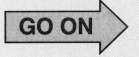

30 The setting of this story is important because it helps the reader understand that—

A differences between people and places create conflicts

B Wolfert Webber's cabbage farm provided a hard life

C the town was growing

D New York was a Dutch colony

31 What problem does Wolfert face?

A He isn't satisfied with his income as a cabbage farmer.

B His daughter wants to marry a poor man.

C His wife complains when he ruins the fields.

D He doesn't believe his friends.

32 Read this passage.

> An old Dutch governor once owned the orchard. He buried the gold on a night when the moon was full.

This is an example of—

A figure of speech

B flashback

C problem resolution

D purpose

33 Paragraph 5 is an example of—

A foreshadowing

B plot

C setting

D theme

34 How is Wolfert similar to most of his neighbors?

A He believes pirate stories.

B He digs up his farm.

C He is a farmer.

D He spends all his savings.

35 What word describes Dirk's mood in paragraph 11?

A angry

B complaining

C concerned

D lonely

36 The author's use of third-person point of view helps the reader learn—

A how Amy and Dirk first meet

B what Wolfert finds buried along the river

C who the scarred stranger really is

D why Wolfert wants to be rich

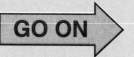
GO ON

Strategies for Test-Taking Success: Reading © Thomson Heinle

37 Which words from the passage have nearly OPPOSITE meanings?

A prosperous, wealthy

B orchard, farm

C jealous, admired

D go to, inherit

38 How is Wolfert's problem solved?

A He digs up a chest of pirate gold.

B The farm becomes valuable.

C Amy marries a rich man.

D Dirk saves him from a pirate.

39 Which sentence describes part of the plot?

A Wolfert doesn't always make wise decisions.

B Wolfert was jealous of the rich people from town.

C The story has a happy ending.

D The Webber family lives on a farm outside of town.

40 Why was the town planning a new road?

A The city was expanding.

B Farmers like to drive fast.

C Rich people wanted to build bigger houses.

D The lawyer recommended it.

41 Read this sentence.

> His neighbors said that Wolfert now grew money instead of cabbages.

This is an example of a—

A metaphor

B simile

C personification

D flashback

42 Which statement best states the theme of this story?

A Sometimes the best things in life are in your own backyard.

B A man tries many foolish ways to get rich.

C Don't follow the advice of strangers.

D Always plan ahead.

STOP. THIS IS THE END OF CUMULATIVE PRACTICE TEST 1.
SEE PAGE 179 FOR ANSWERS AND EXPLANATIONS.

Cumulative Practice Test 2

Mark your answers on the Answer Grid.

Read this speech before answering Questions 1 through 7.

	My Notes
VOTE FOR LARA VELEZ **For Student Council President** 1 Woodland School is undergoing many changes. We see it all around us. The size of the student body grew 30 percent in the last three years. The school becomes more diverse every day. We have kids and teachers from every possible background. There's an amazing mix of different races, cultures, and religions. 2 But something is happening at Woodland that we have to deal with. More and more of us only hang out with kids who are just like us. We stick with our own group and never spend time with anyone else. We don't sit together in the cafeteria or in classes. We often don't even know each other's names. It just isn't right. So what are we going to do about it?	

(Continued on next page)

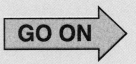

3   Sure, I can be like the other candidates for student council president. I can promise you better food at lunch, more school trips to great places, and popular bands at school dances. And believe me, I'm willing to try to get those things for us.

4   But that's not why I want you to vote for me. I want you to vote for me because I want to make a real difference. I want Woodland to be a place where *everyone* knows your name. If we know each other, we can organize events that previous classes never even thought of. We can work together to have a bigger effect on the community. We can have more school spirit. And we can also have a lot more fun.

5   Members of the Theater Group: What about doing an African comedy, an Asian tragedy, and an American musical by inviting the African American Club, the Asian American Club, and the chorus to help out on *all* of them?

6   Students in the Computer Club: What about repairing used computers to give to senior citizens from different ethnic communities and teaching them how to use them?

7   Athletes: What about starting up *new* teams? What about learning sports that kids play in other countries?

8   And those of you from Asia, Europe, and the Caribbean: Where's that food festival we're all so hungry for?

9   These are just a few of my ideas, and maybe they aren't the best. I just want people to start thinking. We can put our heads together to see what we come up with. If you elect me, I will meet with all the clubs and school groups to see what they think. I'll meet with kids who aren't involved in anything and try to find out why and what their ideas are.

10   I want to be the president of everyone, not just of the kids who run the clubs and get involved in student government. I want to know as many people's names as I can. And I want you to know mine: Lara Velez. Thank you for your vote.

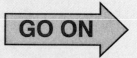

1 What is the purpose of this speech?

A to inform

B to persuade

C to entertain

D to express an opinion

2 In paragraph 1, the word *diverse* means—

A alike

B large

C poetic

D varied

3 Here are four definitions of the word *stick* as they appear in the dictionary. Which definition matches the word's use in paragraph 2?

A a long, thin piece of wood

B a cane

C to puncture with a pointed tool

D to stay with

4 Which of the following is the best restatement of paragraph 2?

A Woodland School has a problem. Groups of students are isolated from each other.

B Students don't know each other's names. It's hard to take attendance.

C The cafeteria is too small for everyone to sit alone at lunch.

D We need to sit facing each other at lunch and in classes.

5 Based on this speech, the listener can infer that Lara Velez—

A doesn't care about school trips or dances

B has most of the answers to problems at Woodland School

C believes things can be better at Woodland School

D belongs to many school clubs

6 In paragraph 4, what does *previous* mean?

A after

B before

C freshman

D next

7 Which BEST describes the central message of this speech?

A Students can find many ways to get closer to each other.

B It's up to each group to make the school different.

C Student council presidents don't really want to make big changes.

D Learning each other's names is a hard thing to do.

GO ON

The Call of the Wild[3]

My Notes

1   John Thornton owned the sled dog Buck. He said that Buck could draw a sled loaded with one thousand pounds of flour. Matthewson bet sixteen hundred dollars that he couldn't. Even though Thornton was afraid it would be too much for Buck, he was ashamed to refuse. So he let Buck try to draw a load that a team of ten dogs was hauling.

2   The miner's team of ten dogs was unhitched. Buck, in his own harness, was put into the sled. The dog felt the general excitement. He felt that in some way, he must do a great thing for John Thornton. Murmurs of admiration at his splendid appearance went up. He was in perfect condition.

3   Thornton knelt down by Buck's side. He took Buck's head into his hands and rested his cheek on Buck's cheek. He whispered in his ear, "As you love me, Buck. As you love me." Then Thornton got to his feet. Buck seized Thornton's hand between his jaws. The dog pressed with his teeth and released slowly. It was his way of answering, not with speech, but with love.

4   Thornton stepped well back. "Now, Buck!" he said.

[3] Adapted from Jack London, *The Call of the Wild*.

GO ON

5   Thornton's command cracked out like a pistol shot. Buck threw himself forward. His whole body was gathered tightly together in a tremendous effort. The dog's muscles twisted and knotted like living things under his silky fur. His great chest was low to the ground, his head was forward and down. His feet were flying like mad. His claws scarred the hard-packed snow in grooves. The sled swayed and trembled, then half-started forward. One of Buck's feet slipped, and one of the men watching groaned aloud. Then the sled lurched ahead in what appeared to be a rapid succession of jerks, though it really never came to a dead stop again. First, half an inch—an inch—two inches . . . The sled gained momentum until it was moving steadily along.

6   Men gasped and began to breathe again, unaware that for a moment they had stopped breathing. Thornton ran behind the sled, encouraging Buck with short, cheery words. The distance for the race was a hundred yards. As Buck neared the end, a cheer began to grow and grow. It burst into a roar as the dog passed the finish line and halted at Thornton's command. Everyone threw mittens and hats in the air, even Matthewson, who had lost his wager. Men were shaking hands and bubbling over in a general incoherent babble. But Thornton fell on his knees beside Buck. Head was against head, and he was shaking him back and forth. Tears were streaming down his cheeks

My Notes

---

8 **What is the main idea of the excerpt?**

  A A dog makes a great effort for the owner it loves.

  B A dog struggles to pull a heavy sled.

  C A miner's camp is excited about a dog race.

  D Two miners make a bet.

9 **In paragraph 1, what does the word *draw* mean?**

  A illustrate

  B pick

  C pull

  D tie

10 **Read this passage.**

> The dog felt the general excitement. He felt that in some way, he must do a great thing for John Thornton.

This is an example of—

  A conflict resolution

  B flashback

  C foreshadowing

  D mood

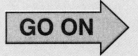

GO ON

11 Why does John Thornton take Buck's head into his hands, rest his cheek on the dog's cheek, and whisper, "As you love me, Buck. As you love me."?

A Thornton believes Buck's love for him will make the dog strong.

B Thornton tries to convince Buck that he can beat the other team of dogs.

C Thornton shows Buck who is boss.

D Thornton wants to show the other miners what a good dog owner he is.

12 In paragraph 5, the author writes:

> Thornton's command cracked out like a pistol shot.

Using words this way is an example of—

A metaphor

B personification

C plot

D simile

13 Which happened last?

A Buck's paws claw at the ice.

B Matthewson's dog team is unhitched.

C The sled moves forward an inch.

D Thornton gives Buck a command.

14 Complete this analogy:
yell : whisper :: roar : _____

A babble

B command

C murmur

D words

15 The author's use of the third-person point of view helps the reader understand—

A why John Thornton makes the bet with Matthewson

B how Buck looks and acts waiting for Thornton's command

C how the men feel about Buck's success

D all of the above

16 The author probably wrote this story to—

A persuade

B influence

C inform

D narrate

17 Which statement BEST summarizes the author's message?

A Dogsled races were a tradition in old mining camps.

B Love and loyalty can overcome great odds.

C People always love a winner.

D Strength and practice are important for winning.

GO ON

Ramirez, Stacey Use Defibrillator, Save Student

1   Yesterday, freshman Yeechee Wang collapsed suddenly in science class. Her life was saved by the quick work of science teacher Jorge Ramirez, school nurse Linda Stacey, and a portable defibrillator.

2   Yeechee Wang suddenly fell to the floor. Mr. Ramirez rushed over. He turned Yeechee over gently. She was hardly breathing. Her pulse was very weak. Mr. Ramirez sent for the nurse. He told a student to call 911 on his cell phone. Then Mr. Ramirez went into action. He tipped Yeechee's head back and started cardiopulmonary resuscitation, or CPR.

3   CPR restores circulation of oxygen-rich blood to the brain. Without oxygen, serious brain damage can occur in less than 8 minutes. No one knew it at the time, but Yeechee was having a heart attack.

4   Ms. Stacey raced to the science lab with the school's automated defibrillator. A defibrillator is a machine that delivers an electric shock to the heart. The shock stops disturbances in the rhythm of the heart. These disturbances can be fatal. But Yeechee was lucky. Last summer, Mr. Ramirez learned how to use a defibrillator. The automated machines are easy to use. You don't need to be an expert, but you do need training.

5   Ms. Stacey took over the CPR while Mr. Ramirez started the defibrillator. "I hooked up the defibrillator and attached the pads to Yeechee," he said. "Then the machine analyzed her condition. It measured her pulse. It sounds incredible, but the automated defibrillator issues audible instructions. An electronic voice tells you what to do."

6   The machine said that Yeechee needed an electric shock. After the first shock, the defibrillator said it was time to start CPR again. Ramirez and Stacey followed the machine's instructions. After a short period of CPR, the defibrillator said another shock was needed. So a second shock was administered. More CPR followed.

7   Soon the emergency medical technicians (EMTs) arrived. They gave Yeechee oxygen. The defibrillator called for another shock. "After that," said Ramirez, "Yeechee started breathing, and the machine detected a faint pulse." One of the EMTs said, "Without that machine, the girl would not have survived." The EMTs then took Yeechee to South Street Hospital. Her parents report that she is in good condition and wants to get back to school.

(Continued on next page)

The letters in CPR stand for **c**ardio**p**ulmonary **r**esuscitation. Classes are available just about everywhere, so take one. It could save a life.

Steps in CPR

It's as easy as **ABC.**
A is for **Airway**

- Place the victim flat on his/her back.
- Shake the victim gently by the shoulders. Shout, "Are you okay?"
- No response: Call an emergency medical team (911).
- Open the victim's airway by tilting his/her head back with one hand. Lift his/her chin with your other hand.

B is for **Breathing**

- Position your cheek close to the victim's nose and mouth. Look toward the victim's chest.
- Look, listen, and feel for any breathing.
- No breathing: pinch his/her nose closed. Give 2 full breaths into his/her mouth.
- Breaths are blocked: reposition the victim's head and try again.
- Breaths still blocked: perform the Heimlich maneuver (stomach presses) to make sure nothing is stuck in the victim's mouth.

C is for **Circulation**

- Check for the victim's pulse by feeling the side of the victim's neck.
- No breathing: give "rescue breathing."
- No pulse: begin chest presses. Put the heel of one of your hands on the lower part of the victim's chest. With your other hand directly on top of your first hand, depress the chest 1.5 to 2 inches.
- Perform 15 presses for every 2 breaths.
- Check for a pulse every minute.

Continue CPR uninterrupted until advanced   life support is available.

—L. Chavez

18 **From the article, what can you tell about heart attack victims?**

A   They can be any age.

B   They all get three shocks from defibrillators.

C   They own personal defibrillators.

D   They all need CPR.

19 **CPR saves lives because it—**

A   stops all brain damage

B   isn't fatal

C   prevents heart attacks

D   sends blood to the brain

GO ON

20 What does the word *circulation* mean in this sentence?

> CPR restores circulation of oxygen-rich blood to the brain.

A change

B flow

C spread

D readership

21 Read this part of the article:

> It sounds incredible, but the automated defibrillator issues audible instructions.

In this sentence, what does *incredible* mean?

A disagreeable

B illegal

C inactive

D unbelievable

22 Which word comes from the Latin root meaning "sound"?

A attach

B attack

C audible

D automate

23 What effect does the automated defibrillator have on heart attack victims?

A It connects them to 911.

B It administers CPR.

C It shocks the heart back into a steady beat.

D It sends for EMTs.

24 What is the main idea of paragraph 5 in the article?

A Defibrillators work best when they give audible instructions.

B Mr. Ramirez attaches pads to Yeechee.

C Ms. Stacey and Mr. Ramirez work as a team.

D The defibrillator provides important information on Yeechee's condition.

25 *Before* Mr. Ramirez administered CPR on Yeechee, he—

A attached the defibrillator pads

B gave her heart a shock

C had a student call the emergency medical number

D talked with the school nurse

GO ON ⟶

26 **Which sentence shows an opinion?**

   A Mr. Ramirez can use a defibrillator.

   B Ms. Stacey is trained in CPR.

   C Yeechee is lucky.

   D EMTs have oxygen for emergencies.

27 **Mr. Ramirez followed all the steps in "A is for Airway" in the boxed sidebar, EXCEPT—**

   A Place the victim flat on his/her back.

   B Shake the victim gently by the shoulders. Shout, "Are you okay?"

   C No response: Call an emergency medical team (911).

   D Open the victim's airway by tilting his/her head back with one hand. Lift his/her chin with your other hand.

28 **The information box is mainly intended to—**

   A prevent heart attacks

   B outline simple emergency care

   C give a complete course on CPR

   D take the place of a defibrillator

29 **Choose the best summary of the information box.**

   A Learn these ABCs to help you remember the steps in CPR.

   B Check the victim's pulse frequently.

   C Lay the victim on his/her back and try to get his/her attention. If the victim is not breathing, call 911. Then try to get air into his/her lungs.

   D The Heimlich maneuver helps unblock airways.

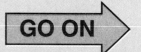

The Creation of Man[4]
A Legend from the Miwok Tribe

1   After Coyote completed making the world, he thought about creating Man. He called a council of all the animals. The animals sat in a circle, with Lion at the head. On Lion's right was Grizzly Bear; next was Cinnamon Bear; and so on down to Mouse, who sat at Lion's left.

2   Lion spoke first. "I wish Man to have a terrible voice, like myself. Then he can frighten all animals." Lion also wanted Man to be well covered with hair and have sharp claws and very strong teeth.

3   Grizzly Bear laughed. "It's ridiculous to have a voice like Lion," he said. "His roar frightens away the prey he is hunting. But Man," said Grizzly Bear, "must have very great strength. He should move silently, but very swiftly. He should seize his prey without noise."

4   Deer agreed that a terrible voice was absurd. But Deer thought that Man would look foolish without a fine set of antlers. Mountain Sheep said antlers get in the way when you're caught in a thicket. Beaver said Man needs a tail. "But it should be broad and flat, so he can haul mud and sand on it," said Beaver. "And I do not recommend a furry tail, which is troublesome on account of fleas," he explained.

5   Owl said Man would be useless without wings. But Mole said wings would be folly. Man would be sure to bump against the sky. Besides, if he had both wings and eyes, he would get his eyes burned by flying too near the sun. Mole declared, "However, without eyes, Man can burrow deep in the soft, cool earth. There, Man will be happy." Mouse said that Man needed eyes so he could see what he is eating. "Nobody wants to burrow in the damp earth, anyway," said Mouse. Other animals murmured, "True enough."

6   When it came to Coyote's turn, he said that the other animals were foolish. "Why do you want Man to be just like you?" he asked. "I want my creation to look better than I do. And certainly, better looking than any of you!" Coyote added, "Of

(Continued on next page)

[4] Adapted from Katharine Berry Judson, "The Creation of Man" in *Myths and Legends of California and the Old Southwest* (Lincoln: University of Nebraska Press, 1994).

GO ON ⟹

course, Man needs four legs and five fingers. Man needs a strong voice, but he doesn't have to roar all the time with it." Looking around, Coyote considered the other animals present. "Man's feet should be nearly like Grizzly Bear's so he can stand erect when he needs to. Deer, your eyes and ears are good, even if your antlers aren't. I'll give those to Man, too. Owl has no tail, and Man doesn't need one either," said Coyote. "Man should not have fur, because fur is a burden most of the year. But no animal is as cunning and crafty as I am, so Man should have my wit," Coyote concluded.

7   Then every animal set to work to make Man according to his own idea. Each one took a lump of earth and modeled it to look just like him.

8   All but Coyote, for Coyote began to make the kind of Man he talked about in the council. When the other animals fell asleep, he threw water on their models and spoiled them. Then he worked all night. By morning, his model was finished, and he gave it life long before the others could repair theirs. Thus Man was made by Coyote.

30 At the council, animals sit in order of—

A   age

B   chronology

C   size

D   the alphabet

31 According to Grizzly Bear, Lion doesn't—

A   have strong teeth

B   sit at the head of the circle

C   speak softly

D   speak first

GO ON

32 You can tell that Grizzly Bear—

    A is a quiet hunter

    B has a terrible voice

    C is friends with Deer

    D sits next to Mole

33 Read the sentence.

> **But Deer thought that Man would look foolish without a fine set of antlers.**

This is one of the legend's many examples of—

    A foreshadowing

    B metaphor

    C personification

    D simile

34 Read the passage.

> **But Mole said wings would be folly. Man would be sure to bump against the sky.**

This is an example of—

    A flashback

    B imagery

    C purpose

    D theme

35 What one thing do most animals agree on?

    A Man won't need a tail.

    B Man won't want to live underground.

    C Man won't need five fingers.

    D Man won't have to fly.

36 In paragraph 5, the word *burrow* means—

    A cart

    B dig

    C lend

    D thicket

37 How is Coyote different from the other animals?

    A Coyote wants Man to look just like him.

    B Coyote laughs at the other animals' ideas.

    C Coyote wants Man to have the best of each animal.

    D Coyote goes to sleep at night with the other animals.

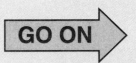
GO ON

38 Read this sentence from the story.

> Of course, Man needs four legs and five fingers.

This is an example of—

A a flashback

B a metaphor

C an inference

D an opinion

39 Coyote is the animal who makes Man because—

A Coyote is cunning and crafty

B Coyote and Grizzly Bear agree that Man needs four feet and no tail

C Lion picks him

D the animals like his ideas best

40 Which words from the passage have nearly OPPOSITE meanings?

A cool, damp

B cunning, foolish

C hair, fur

D made, modeled

41 What is the theme of this story?

A how Man came to be

B when animals cooperate

C how Coyote tricked his friends

D why Man doesn't have a terrible voice

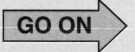

### Building a Castle[5]	**My Notes**

1   In a forest in the French province of Burgundy, a group of men and women are going 800 years back in time. They are building an authentic medieval castle. Nothing is modern. They are using the same tools that people used in the Middle Ages. All the materials for the castle come from the local area.

2   The leader of the project is an historian named Michel. He is an expert on old castles. He even lives in one nearby. It was his idea to build a new castle using old methods. He wanted to test historians' conception of how castles were built long ago.

3   A lot of people help out. The volunteers who work with him come from many places and many walks of life. For example, Katrin was a history student in Germany. Now she makes tiles for the castle's floor. "My parents were shocked at first," she says. "But then they saw my work. I am a real artisan now."

4   "My friends were quite surprised, too," says Meyer. "I was mayor of a small Austrian village. Now I'm a stonemason. I turn boulders into 60-pound blocks for the castle's walls."

5   "I surprised myself," laughs Marie. "I used to sell expensive silk dresses in Paris. Now I cut down trees and saw them into wooden planks."

6   The pace of life at the castle is slow because volunteers like Katrin, Meyer, and Marie make their own tools. It takes time to carve handles for wooden buckets, braid rope, or assemble horse carts. But people there don't mind. They are happy to see walls and towers take shape, even if construction goes on for a long, long time.

7   "Tourists often watch us," Katrin says. "We expect to finish the castle in about 20 years."

8   "That seems so long," says a tourist.

9   "That's nothing," Meyer answers. "It will probably last a thousand."

[5] Based on information at www.guédelon.org.

GO ON

42 Michel is building a castle with old-fashioned methods because—

A he wants to test historians' ideas

B it brings tourists to his little town

C it costs less

D volunteers are excited by the idea

43 You can tell that an *artisan*—

A builds castles

B is skilled

C paints wood floors

D studies history

44 From the passage, the reader can conclude that the walls of the castle are made of—

A brick

B masonry

C stone

D tile

45 What are paragraphs 3 through 6 mainly about?

A Volunteer builders come from different backgrounds.

B Friends and family are unhappy with this project.

C Each volunteer is responsible for a different task.

D Only volunteers from Europe can work on this project.

GO ON

46 **Where is Meyer from?**

A   Paris

B   Germany

C   Burgundy

D   Austria

47 **What sentence best summarizes paragraph 6?**

A   Each volunteer makes special tools for work that is slow but rewarding.

B   The volunteers like to do different kinds of work.

C   The volunteers work very slowly with their tools, so the castle takes a long time to finish.

D   The workers need buckets, rope, and horse carts to build the castle.

48 **Which of these words are closest in meaning?**

A   student, mayor

B   boulders, planks

C   medieval, middle ages

D   saw, turn

49 **Complete this analogy.**
carve: wooden handles :: sew : _____

A   silk dresses

B   floor tiles

C   braided rope

D   fine stitching

50 **Which definition represents the meaning of the word *last* as used in paragraph 9 of the reading?**

A   final

B   one before

C   one remaining

D   survive

51 **When do these events take place?**

A   800 years ago

B   in the Middle Ages

C   several years ago

D   in the present

**STOP. THIS IS THE END OF CUMULATIVE PRACTICE TEST 2.
SEE PAGE 183 FOR ANSWERS AND EXPLANATIONS.**

Chapter 7

Get the Best Score

Sun	Mon	Tue	Wed	Thu	Fri	Sat
	1 Today: Make a plan	2 5:00–6 Study time	3 5:00–6 Study time	4 5:00–6 Study time	5 5:00–6 Study time	6 5:00–6 Study time
7	8 5:00–6 Study time	9 5:00–6 Study time	10 Study for science test	11 5:00–6 Study time	12 5:00–6 Study time	13 5:00–6 Study time
14	15 5:00–6 Study time	16 5:00–6 Study time	17 5:00–6 Study time	18 5:00–6 Study time	19 Birthday party for Dad	20 5:00–6 Study time
21	22 5:00–6 Study time	23 5:00–6 Study time	24 5:00–6 Study time	25 5:00–6 Study time	26 5:00–6 Study time	27 School play
28	29 4:00–6 Soccer	30 RELAX	31 TEST			

You have studied the skills you need. You have practiced good test-taking strategies. You are ready for the test. Here are some ideas to get you through test week.

Relax. This is a tense week. Be sure to take time to relax and have some fun.

Be positive about your work. Focus on what you know and what you can do.

Get regular physical exercise. Don't forget to balance schoolwork and exercise. Exercise helps your body be stronger. It helps you sleep well, too, so you can learn better.

On the night before the test:

- **Prepare for the test day.** Organize things you need for the test. Here is a sample list:
  - ✓ sharpened pencils and erasers
  - ✓ a pen, paper
  - ✓ fruit or other healthy snacks for breaks
  - ✓ eyeglasses
  - ✓ watch
  - ✓ a sweater or sweatshirt (in case the room is cold)

- **Eat dinner.** Drink a glass of milk, too. The calcium in milk relaxes you naturally.

- **Relax and don't study.** Cramming (studying at the last minute) doesn't help. It just makes you worry.

- **Set the alarm.** You don't want to be late for school. Get a good night's sleep.

On the morning of the test:

- **Eat breakfast.** You can't do your best without it!

During the test:

- **Focus on your work.** Don't waste time worrying or wondering how other people are doing. Don't worry about what you did before or what may happen in the future. Pay attention to **what you can do now**.

- **Ask questions.** If you don't understand the directions or if you aren't sure about what you are supposed to do, ask the teacher.

- **Answer the easy questions first.** Then go back and try the hard ones. Don't spend a lot of time on one question. You want enough time to finish the whole test.

- **Always make a guess.** Pick the best answer you can. Use the **process of elimination** to help you guess. If you still have blanks, pick one letter and mark any blanks left with that letter.

Good Luck!

Glossary

Analogy is a relationship or connection between word pairs.

Antonyms are words with opposite meanings.

Author's purpose is the reason for writing.

Cause and effect A cause *makes* something happen. An effect is *what* happens.

Characters are people or animals in a story.

Chronology is time order.

Compare is to find what is *alike* or the *same*.

Compound word is two small words put together to form a third, new word.

Connotative meaning is the feeling, image, or figurative meaning of a word.

Contrast is to find what is *different* or *dissimilar.*

Denotative meaning is the dictionary, factual, or literal meaning of a word.

Fact and opinion A fact can be proved. It is real information. An opinion is what a person thinks or believes. It may or may not be real.

Flashback is an event that happens *before* the story begins, but is described *after* the story starts.

Foreshadowing is a clue or hint about an event later in the story.

Graphic aids show information, or data. Tables, flowcharts, graphs, and maps are graphic aids.

Homonyms are words that sound alike but have different meanings and different spellings.

Imagery makes a picture in your mind, usually using your five senses.

Inference is a reasonable guess you can make about information in a reading. Making an inference is similar to drawing a conclusion.

Main idea is the most important idea in a reading. It is a *general statement*.

Metaphor is a comparison.

Mood is the feeling a reader gets from a story or poem.

Multiple-meaning words have more than one meaning. The specific definition is determined by context.

Paraphrase is to retell a passage in your own words, including the main idea and important details.

Personification shows human feelings or actions in animals or things.

Plot is the events or actions of a story. The plot usually follows a sequence.

Point of view is how the narrator sees and tells the story.

Prefix is a word part added to the beginning of a word. It adds meaning to the root.

Problem resolution is the outcome or conclusion of a story.

Process of elimination is a method for improving guessing in multiple-choice questions.

Root is the part of a word with the main meaning.

Sequence is the order of events.

Setting shows the time and place of a story.

Simile uses *like* or *as* to compare.

Suffix is a word part added to the end of a word. It adds meaning to the root.

Summarize is to find and describe the most important ideas in a passage. It's similar to stating the main idea.

Supporting detail is a fact, example, or explanation that helps you understand the main idea. It is specific, not general.

Synonyms are words with similar meanings.

Theme is the central idea, lesson, or message of a story.

Words in context is a vocabulary strategy for figuring out the meaning of new words from the words around them.

Words often confused are words that sound or look alike but have different meanings and spellings.

Glosario

Analogy (Analogía) Relación o conexión entre pares de palabras.

Antonyms (Antónimos) Palabras con significados opuestos.

Author's purpose (Propósito del autor) La razón que tiene el autor para escribir.

Cause and effect (Causa y efecto) Una causa *hace* que algo suceda. Un efecto es *lo que* sucede.

Characters (Personajes) Personas o animales de una historia.

Chronology (Cronología) El arreglo de eventos, fechas, periodos, etc. en el orden en que suceden.

Compare (Comparar) Identificar lo *que se parece* o lo que es *lo mismo*.

Compound word (Palabra compuesta) Está formada por la unión de dos palabras cortas.

Connotative meaning (Significado connotativo) Sentimiento, imagen o significado figurativo de una palabra.

Contrast (Contrastar) Comparar palabras, cosas, etc. para encontrar lo que es *diferente* o *distinto* entre ellas.

Denotative meaning (Significado denotativo) Es el significado que aparece en el diccionario, el que se basa en los hechos o el literal de una palabra.

Fact and opinion (Hecho y opinión) Un hecho puede probarse, es información real. Una opinión es lo que una persona piensa o cree. Puede ser real o no.

Flashback (Escena retrospectiva) Algo que sucedió *antes* de que la historia comience, pero que se describe *después* de que la historia comienza.

Foreshadowing (Prefiguración) Pista o insinuación indirecta sobre un evento posterior en la historia.

Graphic aids (Ayudas gráficas) Muestran información o datos. Las tablas, flujogramas, gráficos y mapas son ayudas gráficas.

Homonyms (Homónimos) Palabras que suenan igual pero que tienen significado y escritura diferentes.

Imagery (Imágenes) Representaciones mentales basadas en el texto, tal como las crea la imaginación.

Inference (Inferencia) Suposición razonable que puedes hacer con base en la información en una lectura. Hacer una inferencia es similar a llegar a una conclusión.

Main idea (Idea principal) La idea más importante en una lectura. Es una *afirmación general*.

Metaphor (Metáfora) Es una comparación.

Mood (Humor) Sentimiento que el lector obtiene de una historia o poema.

Multiple-meaning words (Palabras con varios significados) Son palabras que tienen más de un sentido. El sentido específico se determina por el contexto.

Paraphrase (Parafrasear) Repetir un pasaje con tus propias palabras, incluyendo la idea principal y los detalles importantes.

Personification (Personificación) Muestra sentimientos o acciones humanos en animales o cosas.

Plot (Argumento o trama) Son los eventos o acciones de una historia. Por lo general el argumento sigue una secuencia.

Point of view (Punto de vista) Es la manera en que el narrador ve y cuenta la historia.

Prefix (Prefijo) Sílaba o grupo de sílabas que se agrega al inicio de una palabra. Le añade significado a esa palabra o raíz.

Problem resolution (Resolución del problema) El desenlace o conclusión de una historia.

Process of elimination (Proceso de eliminación) Método para mejorar el proceso de acierto en preguntas de opción múltiple.

Root (Raíz) Parte de la palabra que contiene el significado principal.

Sequence (Secuencia) Es el orden de los hechos.

Setting (Situación) El tiempo, el lugar, las circunstancias, etc. de una historia.

Simile (Símil) Usa la palabra *como* para comparar.

Suffix (Sufijo) Sílaba o grupo de sílabas que se agrega al final de una palabra. Añade significado a esa palabra o raíz.

Summarize (Resumir) Identificar y presentar las ideas más importantes de un pasaje. Es parecido a describir la idea principal.

Supporting detail (Detalle de apoyo) Hecho, ejemplo o explicación que ayuda a que entiendas la idea principal. Es específico, no general.

Synonyms (Sinónimos) Palabras con significado igual o casi igual.

Theme (Tema) Idea, lección o mensaje central de una historia.

Words in context (Palabras en contexto) Estrategia de vocabulario que busca el significado de palabras nuevas usando las palabras que las acompañan.

Words often confused (Palabras que se confunden frecuentemente) Son palabras que se ven o suenan parecido, pero que tienen significado y escritura diferentes.

Index

INDEX

ANSWER GRID

Print your name in the boxes. Blacken the circle under each letter.

| LAST NAME | FIRST NAME | MI |

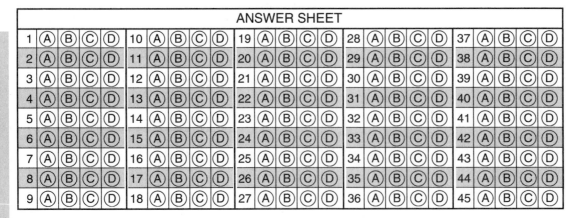

STUDENT ID NUMBER

DIRECTIONS

Use a number 2 pencil

Darken circles completely

Examples:

Wrong ⊘

Wrong ⊗

Wrong ◕

Right ●

ANSWER SHEET

1 Ⓐ Ⓑ Ⓒ Ⓓ	10 Ⓐ Ⓑ Ⓒ Ⓓ	19 Ⓐ Ⓑ Ⓒ Ⓓ	28 Ⓐ Ⓑ Ⓒ Ⓓ	37 Ⓐ Ⓑ Ⓒ Ⓓ
2 Ⓐ Ⓑ Ⓒ Ⓓ	11 Ⓐ Ⓑ Ⓒ Ⓓ	20 Ⓐ Ⓑ Ⓒ Ⓓ	29 Ⓐ Ⓑ Ⓒ Ⓓ	38 Ⓐ Ⓑ Ⓒ Ⓓ
3 Ⓐ Ⓑ Ⓒ Ⓓ	12 Ⓐ Ⓑ Ⓒ Ⓓ	21 Ⓐ Ⓑ Ⓒ Ⓓ	30 Ⓐ Ⓑ Ⓒ Ⓓ	39 Ⓐ Ⓑ Ⓒ Ⓓ
4 Ⓐ Ⓑ Ⓒ Ⓓ	13 Ⓐ Ⓑ Ⓒ Ⓓ	22 Ⓐ Ⓑ Ⓒ Ⓓ	31 Ⓐ Ⓑ Ⓒ Ⓓ	40 Ⓐ Ⓑ Ⓒ Ⓓ
5 Ⓐ Ⓑ Ⓒ Ⓓ	14 Ⓐ Ⓑ Ⓒ Ⓓ	23 Ⓐ Ⓑ Ⓒ Ⓓ	32 Ⓐ Ⓑ Ⓒ Ⓓ	41 Ⓐ Ⓑ Ⓒ Ⓓ
6 Ⓐ Ⓑ Ⓒ Ⓓ	15 Ⓐ Ⓑ Ⓒ Ⓓ	24 Ⓐ Ⓑ Ⓒ Ⓓ	33 Ⓐ Ⓑ Ⓒ Ⓓ	42 Ⓐ Ⓑ Ⓒ Ⓓ
7 Ⓐ Ⓑ Ⓒ Ⓓ	16 Ⓐ Ⓑ Ⓒ Ⓓ	25 Ⓐ Ⓑ Ⓒ Ⓓ	34 Ⓐ Ⓑ Ⓒ Ⓓ	43 Ⓐ Ⓑ Ⓒ Ⓓ
8 Ⓐ Ⓑ Ⓒ Ⓓ	17 Ⓐ Ⓑ Ⓒ Ⓓ	26 Ⓐ Ⓑ Ⓒ Ⓓ	35 Ⓐ Ⓑ Ⓒ Ⓓ	44 Ⓐ Ⓑ Ⓒ Ⓓ
9 Ⓐ Ⓑ Ⓒ Ⓓ	18 Ⓐ Ⓑ Ⓒ Ⓓ	27 Ⓐ Ⓑ Ⓒ Ⓓ	36 Ⓐ Ⓑ Ⓒ Ⓓ	45 Ⓐ Ⓑ Ⓒ Ⓓ

Strategy 3, page 24

1. **A.** It is general. It is a good topic sentence.
B and **C** are details.
2. **A.** explanation. This is a *reason* the Gomez triplets like the convention.
B. fact. It is a detail. It answers *How many?*
C. example. This is an example of people's questions about triplets.

Strategy 4, page 27

Practice A alphabetical; file A–D, E–J, K–O, U–Z
Practice B 1. *last* 2. *first* 3. *Next* 4. *At noon*
5. *Before lunch* 6. *in the afternoon* 7. *at 10 o'clock*

8:00 science	12:00 lunch
9:00 English	1:30 history
10:00 math	2:30 Latin
11:00 band	

Strategy 5, page 29

Practice A 1. CP/also
2. CT/however
Practice B Answers will vary.

Strategy 6, page 32

Practice A 1. Mt. McKinley/table, graph
2. Alaska/flowchart 3. Vera Cruz/flowchart
4. Pacific/map 5. Logan/graph
Practice B 1. both 2. instead 3. similarly
4. but

1. (C)
A This is a detail.
B False. The National Mall is a park, not a shopping mall.
C *Main idea* (signal: *mainly about*)
This answer has general information from both paragraphs.
D Use paragraph numbers. The stem points to the paragraphs 1 and 2. This information is in paragraph 5.

2. (A)
A *Graphic aid: legend*
The numbers are like a legend.
B No information in the reading.
C There is no information about *correct order*.
D The map is a guide for visitors, not the National Park Service.

3. (C)
A and B No information in the reading.
C *Graphic aid: map and flowchart*
The Washington Monument is the only place directly between the Lincoln Memorial and the Capitol.
D The Smithsonian Air and Space Museum is on the side of the mall.

4. (B)
A, C, and D are far from each other. A is 1-2-6, C is 6-5-3, and D is 5-3-1.
B *Graphic aid: map* Each number is a place in the brochure. The places in B are closest: 3-4-2.

5. (C)
A, B, and D There *is* information in the brochure.
C *Supporting detail* There is *no* information in the brochure about when *Apollo 11* landed on the moon.

ANSWER KEY CHAPTER 2

6. (C)

A   Alike. The Vietnam Veterans Memorial is made of granite, too.

B   There is no information in the reading about who designed other memorials.

C   *Contrast* (signal: *different from*) There are no heroes in battle in the Vietnam Veterans Memorial.

D   False. Some people *called* it *a black scar.*

7. (A)

A   *Sequence* (signal: *last*)
People still search the wall today. It is present-day information.

B, C, and D are all in the past.

8. (B)

A, B, and D   Alike. All show strong feelings—sadness or anger.

B   *Contrast* (signal: *All/except*)
It is a fact. It doesn't show feelings.

9. (A)

A   *Compare* (signal: *both*)
Alike. Both readings say the wall is black.

B and D   Different. This information is only in the brochure.

C   Different. This information is only in the biography note.

10. (D)

A   This is about a detail.

B   No information in the reading.

C   The passage is not about Mary Shelley. It's about her book.

D   *Main idea* (signal: *good title*)
This is a general idea. It answers: *What is this reading about?*

11. (C)

A   No information in the reading.

B   No information in the reading.

C   *Contrast* (signal: *different from*)
The signal word *But* shows contrast: *Before Frankenstein, there was no use of science in horror stories. But Dr. Frankenstein was a man of science.*

D   False. Paragraph 1 says: *There are over 250 editions today.*

12. (A)

A   *Compare* (signal: *like*)
Alike. This is in paragraph 1.

B   Different. Today's horror movies are scary.

C   No information about who writes today's movies.

D   No information in the reading.

13. (B)

A and D came after *Frankenstein.*

B   *Sequence* (signal: *first*)
Before Frankenstein, *there was no use of science in horror stories.* There were already scary stories.

C   *Frankenstein* was the first science fiction book. Horror stories came before it.

CHAPTER 3
Practices Strategies 7–10
Answers and Explanations

Strategy 7, page 41

Practice A 2. A/consequently 3. D/As a result of 4. B/so
Practice B Answers will vary.

Strategy 8, pages 44–45

Practice A 1. True; Hints: *milk, cereal, yogurt, peanut butter, cart, in line*
2. False; Hint: *lunchbox* probably means Manuel is a child, not a cashier
3. False; The speaker isn't shopping from a list.
4. True; Hint: *Oh, look! Hmmm.* and *Oh no!* show the speaker's words or thoughts.
Practice B 1. B 2. A 3. A

Strategy 9, pages 47–48

Practice A 1. Opinion 2. Opinion 3. Fact
4. Fact 5. Opinion 6. Fact 7. Opinion
Practice B
1. *Tree frogs are a* beautiful *color.*
2. I think *bats are helpful.*
3. *They are* cute and shy.
4. *Army ants are* nasty *bugs.*
5. *But* it's easy to see *why they grow fast.*
Practice C Answers will vary.

Strategy 10, page 50

Practice A 1. D 2. B
Practice B Sample answers:
Summary—Zoovia and the writer train together in different towns for the Boston Marathon.
Paraphrase—Zoovia and the writer are training for the Boston Marathon. They run every day. They run in different cities. They will soon run up a very hard hill. Then they will be ready to run all 26 miles.

Photocopying this page is prohibited by law.

CHAPTER 3
Review Test
Answers and Explanations
Pages 51–59

 1. (C)
A This is about a detail.
B This is too general. It doesn't talk about kites.
C *Main idea* (signal: *best title*)
This answer is a good, general title.
D This article gives 6 steps to *make* a kite, not to *do* an activity.

 2. (D)
A, B, and C are true according to the reading. So the passage supports them.
D *Contrast* (signal: *all/except*)
Toy makers are not involved in trade routes. The author does not discuss this choice.

3. (A)
A *Cause and effect* (signal: *because*) Flying is caused by the wind.
B and D No information in the reading.
C The tail keeps the kite from tipping over, but it doesn't lift it up to fly.

4. (C)
A False. The glue has to dry, not the surface.
B No information in the reading.
C *Facts* (signal: *most important fact*)
This is a fact in the reading. *Make sure* shows it is an important fact.
D False. The long stick isn't glued. The string is glued.

5. (D)
A False. The sticks are tied in Step 2.
B False. You tie on the tail in Step 5.
C False. The sticks are laid down before the tape.
D *Make an inference* (signal: *infer*)
Correct. Sentence 3 in Step 4 shows that tape is removed so the paper can be glued to the frame.

6. (A)

A *Paraphrase* (signal: *best restatement*)
This is a different way to say the main idea and important details.

B and C have steps out of sequence and false information.

D This is a summary, not a restatement.

7. (A)

A *Sequence* (signal: *last*)
This is the last part of Step 5.

B and C No information in the reading.

D False. This is done before Step 5.

8. (D)

A, B, and C have other purposes.

D *Supporting detail*
This is stated in Step 5.

9. (C)

A and D False. Weevils "ruined the pasta."

B No information in the reading.

C *Opinion* (signal: *the mother thinks*) The mother's opinion is that the bugs are "horrible."

10. (A)

A *Make an inference* They were part of the hoax so you can infer they were actors.

B False. They were part of the hoax.

C False. Viewers watch a show. They aren't in it.

D No information in the reading.

11. (B)

A False. The TV station didn't make the calls. Viewers did.

B *Paraphrase* (signal: *another way of writing*) This is another way to state the main idea and details.

C and D False.

12. (C)

A, B, and D are facts.

C *Opinion* (signal: *I bet you believe*)
This is the teacher's opinion.

13. (D)

A and B No information in the reading.

C False. The information in this reading describes only one April Fool's Day.

D *Make an inference* (signal: *What can you tell*) You can make this inference from paragraph 8.

14. (B)

A These are two details.

B *Summarize* (signal: *best summary*)
This answer describes the main idea in the reading.

C False. The camera operator did not prove it.

D False. It was not news. It was a hoax.

15. (A)

A *Summarize* (signal: *best sums up*)
This sentence states the general topic of the paragraph.

B, C, and D are details.

16. (C)

A, B, and D No information in the reading.

C *Make an inference* (signal: *conclude*)
Pluto, the Roman god of the underworld, is compared to a "dim dot of light."

17. (D)

A and B False. Pluto is not invisible. You can see it with a telescope.

C No information in the reading.

D *Paraphrase* (signal: *best restatement*)
This sentences states the idea in a different way.

18. (B)

A   Alike. Neptune and Jupiter are cold.

B   *Contrast* (signal: *different from*) This is a difference. Paragraph 4 says: *Pluto rotates in the opposite direction from most the other planets.*

C   Alike. All the planets in the solar system revolve around the sun.

D   Alike. Earth also has only one moon.

19. (B)

A, C, and D   False.

B   *Fact.* Paragraph 4 says: *Your weight on Pluto would be only 1/15 what it is on Earth.*

20. (B)

A   False. The ice does not melt when the nitrogen is frozen.

B   *Cause and effect* (signal: *effect*) The ice melts because Pluto gets close to the sun.

C and D are effects of the ice melting. The question asks for a cause.

 21. (D)

A and C   False.

B   No information in the reading.

D   *Supporting detail*
Paragraph 7 says that Pluto is "one half the size of Mercury."

22. (C)

A   False.

B and D are true, but they are details.

C   *Summarize* (signal: *best summary*)
This says the most important idea in the passage.

CHAPTER 4
Practices Strategies 11–15
Answers and Explanations

Strategy 11, page 63

Practice 1. personification. Sample answer: The author compares the noise of a train to a person in pain. I think the train is very noisy.
2. simile. Sample answer: The author compares the man's feet to shovels. I think his feet are very big.
3. personification. Sample answer: The poet makes March into a visitor. I think the poet is happy to see her visitor.
4. metaphor. Sample answer: The author compares Alice to a rose with thorns. I think Alice has good and bad points.

Strategy 12, page 66

Practice A 1. they, she; 3rd person
2. he, it, she; 3rd person
3. I, we; 1st person
4. it, them; 3rd person
5. I; 1st person
Practice B 1. A 2. C 3. B. 4. B

Strategy 13, page 69

Practice A 1. 3; 2. 2, 5; 3. 6, 7
Practice B Sample answers:
1. The lion is tied up with strong ropes.
2. She chews the ropes and frees the lion.

Strategy 14, pages 73–74

Practice A Sample answers:
1. happy
2. laugh
3. a smiling roof
4. the gables laugh
5. hearing

Photocopying this page is prohibited by law.

Practice B
1. foreshadowing 2. flashback 3. flashback
4. foreshadowing

Strategy 15, pages 77–78

Practice 1. B 2. B
3. A 4. B 5. C 6. B

CHAPTER 4
Review Test
Answers and Explanations
Pages 79–85

1. (B)
A, C, and D do not give hints of what is to
  come.
B *Foreshadowing* These are hints of the
  problem to come.

2. (C)
A, B, and D are false.
C *Analyze character* Mathilde's pride does
  not allow her to tell the truth about losing
  the necklace.

3. (D)
A, B, and C do not fit the paragraph.
D *Mood* In this paragraph, Mathilde is sad
  because she looks older, isn't beautiful, and
  had her life changed by a single mistake.

4. (A)
A *Cause and effect* (signal: *because*)
  It's hard to recognize people when they
  look very different.
B, C, and D No information in the reading.

5. (A)
A *Character/inference* Mathilde says her life
  was hard because of Jeanne.
B, C, and D No information in paragraph 7.

6. (D)
A, B, and C The reader learns the information
  in these answers because the narrator is
  outside the story and knows everything that
  happens.
D *Point of view* The narrator outside the story
  tells the reader everything that happens.

7. (D)

A   False. This is a surprise ending, but it is not funny.

B   The author is not trying to persuade the reader of anything.

C   This story is fiction. It does not give facts or explanations.

D   *Purpose* The author tells a story with characters and feelings.

8. (B)

A   Jeanne was a lender without problems.

B   *Theme/summary* Mathilde was too proud to admit she lost the necklace. That caused terrible problems for her.

C   The reader doesn't know if Mathilde will learn and change now that she knows the truth.

D   False. Mathilde did not feel better after 10 years.

9. (D)

A and B   Incorrect. They tell about characters in the story, not plot.

C   Incorrect. This answer tells about point of view, not plot.

D   *Plot* The ending of a story is part of the plot.

10. (A)

A   *Point of view* (signal: *I*)
Most speeches use a first-person point of view.

B   False. The speaker describes a past event but doesn't use it as a hint about the future.

C   False. The speech doesn't have a plot.

D   False. The speaker isn't serious. He makes his point with humor.

11. (C)

A and D are opinions. The signals are: *I think* and *Everyone thought*.

B   Incorrect. This states the man's task or problem.

C   *Problem resolution* This is the outcome of the man's efforts.

12. (B)

A   False. The speaker describes a collector but isn't one himself.

B   *Purpose* The speech is quite silly. The speaker wants to make his audience laugh.

C   False. The speaker doesn't give advice or try to persuade his audience to do anything.

D   False. The speaker made up the "facts" he uses.

13. (B)

A, C, and D are sayings about weather in general, but they don't describe the message of the speech.

B   *Paraphrase* This is a short, clear way of describing what the speaker talks about: the changeable and unpredictable weather of New England.

14. (B)

A   False. There is no sea creature. The mate is describing the violence of the sea.

B   *Main idea* The mate is afraid of the sea. He is losing hope that they will ever see land again.

C   False. The Admiral doesn't speak until line 8. Watch for line numbers.

D   False. You don't read about the "leaping sword" until line 7. Watch for line numbers.

15. (C)

A and B   False. The sea is the opposite of peaceful or calm.

C   *Mood* The sea is very dangerous. The mate says the sea is *mad* and describes it as a monster waiting to bite.

D   No information in the poem.

Photocopying this page is promoted by law.

16. (B)

A   False. The mate talks to the Brave Admiral.

B   *Character* An admiral is the captain of a ship. The title of the poem tells you who this captain is.

C and D   Incorrect. These are not characters.

17. (D)

A and C   No information in the poem.

B   False. This is character motivation, not setting.

D   *Setting* The poet uses the setting to show how difficult the trip was.

18. (B)

A and C   These are descriptions without figures of speech.

B   *Figure of speech* The poet describes the sea with teeth, a curled lip, and ready to bite.

D   This is a quote from Columbus, not a figure of speech.

19. (B)

A   Incorrect. A flashback shows action from the past.

B   *Imagery* The poet makes you "see" the first light of dawn. He uses a metaphor to compare dawn to a flag.

C   Incorrect. The poet does not use *like* or *as,* so the comparison is not a simile.

D   Incorrect. A plot doesn't make a picture in your mind. It shows the action in a story.

20. (C)

A   False. This means the crew must be ready to work.

B   False. There are no sea monsters.

C   *Theme* This is a major theme of the poem. It repeats the earlier call to *Sail on!*

D   No information in the poem.

CHAPTER 5
Practices Strategies 16–21
Answers and Explanations

Strategy 16, page 92

Practice A Sample answers:
1. A shark lives in the ocean.
2. Spanish is a language.
3. Day is the opposite of night.
4. A kitchen is one room in a house.
Practice B 1. B 2. A 3. D 4. A
Practice C 1. D 2. A

Strategy 17, pages 94–95

Practice 1. private 2. refill
3. is dishonest 4. a memory
5. stop 6. easy

Strategy 18, page 99

Practice A 2. b 3. f 4. a
5. h 6. g 7. e 8. c 9. i 10.d
Practice B 1. misunderstand
2. dictator 3. revive
4. century 5. synthesized
6. prediction 7. portable
8. auditorium 9. spectators
10. fearless

Strategy 19, page 102

Practice Circle: 1. tuneful, harmonious 2. like
3. make stronger, fortify, reinforce 4. exhaust
5. foolishness 6. notice 7. undermine 8. single

Strategy 20, pages 106–107

Practice A 1. You're
2. write 3. two
4. week 5. Who's
6. it's 7. No
8. than 9. right
10. weighs 11. except

Practice B A. 4 B. 1 C. 5
D. 3 E. 2
Practice C where; Here's; its; to; piece; It's

Strategy 21, pages 110–112

Practice A Sample answers: 1. synonym:
hardened clay
2. antonym: buried
3. synonym: different; antonym: alike
4. synonym: model
Practice B 1. smaller
2. carried 3. water
Practice C 1. an entry
2. a confirmation 3. an edit

CHAPTER 5
Review Test
Answers and Explanations
Pages 113–118

1. (C)
A, B, and D are definitions of *star* that don't fit
the context.
C *Multiple-meaning words/context* Find *star*
in paragraph 1: *stars of space movies*. Put in
the sentence the four definitions of *star*.
Only *famous* people makes sense.

2. (A)
A *Analogies* Create a bridge sentence, such as,
A **surgeon operates** on patients. A
machinist assembles cars and trucks.
B, C, and D don't make sense in the bridge
sentence.

3. (D)
A, B, and C are definitions of *programs* that
don't fit the context.
D *Multiple-meaning words/technology
vocabulary in context* Find *program* in
paragraph 2. *Every robot is **encoded with a
computer program**. **Programs are sets of
instructions***. These two sentences are
strong context clues that programs are
computer commands.

4. (B)
A, C, and D don't have roots meaning 100.
B *Roots Cent* is a Latin root meaning 100. A
century is 100 years.

5. (B)
A The prefix *bene-* means good. You need a
word about *dangerous work*.
B *Context/roots/prefixes/suffixes* In the
previous sentence, the phrase *dangerous
work* is a strong context clue to look for a
negative word.
C *Healthful* means full of health.
D The root *vi* means life. The suffix *-ous* means
full of. *Vigorous* is full of life or strong.

ANSWER KEY CHAPTER 5

6. (C)

A, B, and D are definitions of *remote* that don't fit the context.

C *Multiple-meaning words/context*
Find *remote* in paragraph 5: *remote operations. Patients are **in other places, sometimes hundreds, or even thousands of miles away.***

7. (A)

A *Context* Hint: **observation** *sensors*. *Observe* means to look or see.

B, C, and D don't fit the context.

8. (C)

A, B, and D don't fit the context

C *Prefixes/context*
The prefix *trans-* means across; the pictures are sent across space.

9. (B)

A Incorrect. The vacuum cleaner helps, but *device* doesn't mean helper.

B *Context/words often confused* The vacuum cleaner is a machine. Here, *device* means machine.

C Incorrect. The word confused here is *devise*, which means to plan.

D Incorrect. The sensor is *part of* the vacuum cleaner.

10. (C)

A and B describe what the vacuum *does*. They do not define *obstacle*.

C *Context* An *obstacle* is something in the way.

D Incorrect. *Chair* is an example in this context, not the meaning.

11. (D)

A is too narrow. A desert is only an example of a habitat.

B Incorrect. It doesn't fit the context.

C is tricky because a *habit* is a routine. It doesn't make sense in the context, however.

D *Context/words often confused* The context describes "grasslands and deserts in Africa and in Asia." Only D is broad enough.

12. (A)

A *Roots/suffixes*
Plenty means a lot; so does the suffix *-ful*.

B and C are antonyms.

D Incorrect. Overflowing means *too* many.

13. (B)

A Alike. These are both continents.

B *Antonyms* These words are opposites, or antonyms.

C Alike. These animals are both food for cheetahs.

D Alike. These are both people who study cheetahs.

14. (C)

A, B, and D are close in meaning. But they don't define the compound word.

C *Compound words/context* The word *caretaker* is made of two smaller words: *care* and *take*. Caretakers raise and protect the young or the weak.

15. (B)

A Incorrect. *Cars* are not *human*.

B *Context* The context: *Poachers sneak . . . to catch them . . . Poachers also hunt . . .* tells that poachers are hunters. They hurt the cheetahs.

C and D Incorrect. These people study cheetahs. They don't harm them.

16. (C)

A Incorrect. Poaching is one way to cook an egg. But the context is wrong.

B and D Sometimes fast drivers and townspeople hurt cheetahs. But these words don't mean harmful.

C *Multiple-meaning words/context*
You can tell that a *poacher* is a robber from context: *Poachers sneak . . . to catch them.*

17. (B)

A Incorrect. The word *refugee* means immigrant.

B *Words often confused/context*
Context hint: *safe.* A refuge is a protected place.

C and D The word *refuse* means to say no or waste or trash.

18. (A)

A *Multiple-meaning words/context* You can tell that track means mark left by something from context: *Scientists know when a cheetah is in an area by its **tracks**. Those large paw prints. . . .*

B, C, and D don't fit the context.

CHAPTER 6
Cumulative Practice Test 1
Answers and Explanations
Pages 127–141

1. (D)

A, B, and C answer setting questions about when and where.

D *Setting* This describes *character*, not setting.

2. (A)

A *Fact* This is a fact. It can be proved.

B and C are opinions about good and bad weather.

D This is about a feeling.

3. (A)

A *Analogy* This analogy shows the person who does an action and the action.

B, C, and D do not fit the meaning of the sentence.

4. (B)

A and D These words are not synonyms. Their context is related.

B *Synonyms* (signal: *closest in meaning*)
These are alike. Both are celebrations.

C is an antonym.

5. (B)

A is only in the schedule.

B *Compare* (signal: *both*) This answer is described in paragraph 2 and in the schedule on Saturday from 2:00–4:00 p.m.

C and D are described only in the reading.

6. (A)

A *Purpose* Schedules provide information, such as time and place.

B There is nothing funny about a schedule.

C and D The schedule does not persuade or influence people to attend a particular event. It provides information so that people can make their own decisions.

Photocopying this page is prohibited by law.

7. (D)

A, B, and C are incorrect.

D *Detail* (signal: *Where*) Find *Alaskan breakfast* on Saturday from 8:00–11:00 a.m.

8. (B)

A, C, and D are incorrect.

B *Sequence and chronology* The boxes show information about the Polar Bear jumpers. The only related activity in the schedule on Saturday between 11:30 and 5:45 is the Polar Bear Plunge at 12:30.

9. (B)

A, C, and D are incorrect.

B *Content-based vocabulary: math* The Polar Bear Parade and Plunge are free to watch ($0). The slippery Salmon Toss is $5. The Dog Show is $2. Haircuts are $25 for any number of people in a family.
$0 + 5 + 2 + 25 = \$32$.

10. (A)

A *Contrast* (signal: *even though*)
This explains the contrast between looking solid and being water.

B, C, and D Read paragraph 1. All these details are true, but they don't explain the contrast between looking solid and being water.

11. (A)

A *Context* You can tell from the passage that ecosystems and environments are synonyms.

B, C, and D don't fit the context.

12. (C)

A, B, and D don't fit the context.

C *Content-based vocabulary: science/context* The definition is given following *comma + or*: *salinity, or salt level.*

13. (A)

A *Cause and effect/context* (signal: *can cause*) This is the only cause.

B, C, and D are not causes.

14. (A)

A *Main idea/summary* (signal: *best summarizes*) This is a general statement about information in the paragraph.

B, C, and D are details.

15. (C)

A and B are true, but they aren't direct effects of draining the wetlands.

C *Cause and effect* Reread paragraph 5 for information.

D No information in the reading.

16. (C)

A, B, and D do not come from the Latin root meaning life.

C *Roots* The Latin root *vita* means life.

17. (B)

A is too broad.

B *Purpose/main idea* This is the main idea of the reading. It could be the basis of a project.

C No information in the reading.

D describes a detail. It is too narrow to be the focus of a project.

18. (D)

A, B, and C make comparisons and use *like* or *as*, so they are similes.

D *Figurative language, contrast* This not a simile.

19. (A)

A *Theme* This is the central idea that the poet wants you to think about.

B The poem does not talk about someone's last morning.

C The poem doesn't talk about the sun.

D The poem asks questions, but not about directions.

20. (A)

A *Point of view* (signal word: *I*)

B, C, and D are incorrect.

21. (C)

A, B, and D Incorrect. There is no indication of any of these feelings in the poem.

C *Mood* The author wonders about many things.

22. (A)

A *Character* The poet calls herself "a little pilgrim."

B, C, and D Incorrect. The poet asks questions of these three and wants them to answer the "little pilgrim."

23. (A)

A *Cause and effect* Reread the section "Background."

B and C No information in the reading.

D False. This describes the new stadium.

24. (A)

A *Main idea* This is a general statement about information in the paragraph.

B False. Seats have different prices.

C and D are true, but they are details.

25. (B)

A, C, and D do not fit the meaning of the sentence.

B *Analogy* This analogy shows pairs of synonyms: *clear–visible* and *blocked–obstructed*. The meaning of *obstructed* is in the context of the section "Background."

26. (B)

A False. The best seats are "closest to home plate and the dugouts." Look at the seating chart to see that "next to the Bullpen" is far from those seats.

B *Graphic aids:seating chart* Look at the seating chart to see that the scoreboard is hard to see from the bleachers.

C False. Reread the paragraph "New Services and look at the seating chart.

D This is an opinion. It can't be proved from the reading or the seating chart.

27. (B)

A, C, and D are definitions of *level* that don't fit the context.

B *Multiple-meaning words* From this sentence you can tell that *level* means height.

28. (C)

A No information in the reading.

B False. The fireworks are electronic. They are seen on the scoreboard.

C *Contrast* (signal: *instead*) Reread the section "New Services."

D False. The scoreboard is *like a giant television*, but it isn't really a television.

29. (C)

A, B, and D are opinions.

C *Fact* This is a fact that can be proved.

30. (A)

A *Setting* The setting introduces the contrast between city life and country life, the rich, farmers, and pirates.

B, C, and D are true, but they don't help to explain the purpose of the setting.

31. (A)

A *Problem identification* This is the problem that leads to Wolfert's struggles.

B and C are true, but they are minor problems that are quickly resolved.

D False. He believes every story he hears.

32. (B)

A Incorrect. There is no use of metaphors, similes, or imagery.

B *Flashback* A flashback shows action from the past that helps explain the present.

C The governor does not solve a problem.

D Incorrect.

33. (A)

A *Foreshadowing* The stranger's appearance is a hint of what will happen later in the story.

B, C, and D are incorrect.

34. (C)

A, B, and D show how Wolfert is different from his neighbors. They think his actions are crazy.

C *Compare/inference* (signal: *similar to*) Wolfert lives in the country. You can infer that his neighbors are farmers, too.

35. (C)

A, B, and D are incorrect. Dirk doesn't show any of these moods or character traits in this paragraph.

C *Mood/character* Dirk shows concern for Wolfert and his wife's fears.

36. (D)

A, B, and C are incorrect. The reader doesn't learn any of this information.

D *Point of view* The narrator outside the story describes the reason Wolfert wants to be rich in paragraph 1.

37. (C)

A, B, and D are pairs of synonyms.

C *Antonyms* (signal: *nearly opposite meanings*)
This pair describes opposite feelings.

38. (B)

A False. Reread paragraph 11.

B *Problem resolution* Remember that Wolfert's problem is that he wants to be rich. He becomes rich not by finding gold, but by selling his valuable land.

C False. Dirk becomes rich *after* he marries Amy.

D Incorrect. The pirate is not Wolfert's main problem.

39. (C)

A Incorrect. This describes character, not plot.

B Incorrect. This describes mood, not plot.

C *Plot* The ending of a story is part of the plot.

D Incorrect. Place is part of setting.

40. (A)

A *Inference* The town was originally small. Now people want to build new homes and shops in the country. You can conclude that the town is getting crowded and needs to expand. Roads are one way towns expand.

B, C, and D There is no information or only partial information in the reading.

41. (A)

A *Figure of speech* In this metaphor, the neighbors compare Wolfert's new wealth to growing cabbages.

B Incorrect. The comparison does not use *like* or *as*.

C Incorrect.

D Incorrect. A flashback tells about action from the past.

42. (A)

A *Theme* This is an important idea that the author wants you to understand.

B is the main idea or summary of the story.

C is about a detail.

D does not describe any idea in the story.

CHAPTER 6
Cumulative Practice Test 2
Answers and Explanations
Pages 143–159

1. (B)

A Incorrect. The speaker is not telling her audience anything new.

B *Purpose* The speaker wants to convince her audience to vote for her.

C Incorrect. The speaker doesn't want to make her audience laugh.

D Incorrect. The speaker is not expressing an opinion.

2. (D)

A, B, and C don't fit the context.

D *Context* Words that provide context are *every possible background* and *an amazing mix of different races, cultures, and religions.*

3. (D)

A, B, and C These definitions don't fit the context.

D *Multiple-meaning words* You can tell from the context that *stick* means stay with.

4. (A)

A *Paraphrase* (signal: *best restatement*) This answer states the main idea and important details in a different way.

B, C, and D have misleading information about the paragraph.

5. (C)

A False. She does care about them.

B False. She says she doesn't have all the answers.

C *Inference* (signal: *infer*) This is why she is running for student council president.

D No information in the speech.

6. (B)

A, C, and D don't fit the context.

B *Prefixes* The prefix *pre-* means before. The speaker is talking about earlier years.

7. (A)

A *Theme* (signal: *central message*) This is what the speaker wants her audience to do. It is the central message of this persuasive speech.

B, C, and D are details, not the central, or important, message.

8. (A)

A *Main idea* This answer describes general information from the whole excerpt.

B, C, and D are all details.

9. (C)

A, B, and D don't fit the context.

C *Multiple-meaning words/context* Find *draw* in paragraph 1: *draw a sled.* Of the four choices, only *pull* makes sense.

10. (C)

A Conflict is not resolved in the passage.

B The passage does not talk about the past.

C *Foreshadowing* This is a hint of the contest to come.

D The dog feels the general excitement of the moment; this does not show his mood.

11. (A)

A *Character* This answer shows the relationship between the man and his dog.

B, C, and D are all false. None of these answers accurately portrays the man or the dog.

12. (D)

A Incorrect. A metaphor does not use *like* to compare.

B Incorrect. This is not personification.

C Incorrect. This is not part of the plot.

D *Simile* (signal: *like*)
This is a simile because it compares the sound of Thornton's command with the sound of a shot using *like*.

13. (C)

A, B, and D all occur before Buck's sled moves.

C *Sequence* (signal: *last*) Reread paragraph 5.

14. (C)

A Babble is nonsense speech; it is not the opposite of *roar*.

B A command is an example of talk; it is not the opposite of *roar*.

C *Analogy/context* Use a bridge sentence such as **Yell *and* whisper *are opposite kinds of loudness*.** The opposite of *roar* is *murmur*.

D You can eliminate *words* because it is not the opposite of roar.

15. (D)

A, B, and C The reader learns the information in these answers because the narrator is outside the story and knows everything that happens.

D *Point of view* The narrator outside the story tells the reader everything that happens.

16. (D)

A and B False. The narrator is not trying to convince the audience to do anything.

C False. The narrator is not providing new information.

D *Purpose* This is fiction with a 3rd person point of view. It is a narrated story.

17. (B)

A, C, and D may be true, but they are not the point of the story.

B *Theme* (signal: author's message)
This is an important idea that the author wants you to understand.

18. (A)

A *Inference* (signal: *what can you tell about*)
You can figure this out because Yeechee Wang is in high school.

B, C, and D have no information in the reading.

19. (D)

A and B No information in the reading.

C False. It is used after heart attacks occur.

D *Cause and effect* (signal: *because*) You are looking for a cause or reason that CPR is valuable. You can find the answer in paragraph 3.

20 (B)

A, C, and D are incorrect.

B *Context/roots/prefixes* The prefix *circu-* means around. The blood flows around the body.

21. (D)

A, B, and C are incorrect.

D *Roots* The Latin root *cred* means believe. The prefix *in-* means not.

22. (C)

A, B, and D are incorrect.

C *Roots* The Latin root *aud* means sound.

23. (C)

A, B, and D are false. People dial 911, administer CPR, and send for EMTs.

C *Cause and effect* This is the main purpose of the machine.

ANSWER KEY CHAPTER 6

24. (D)

A, B, and C are all details.

D *Main idea* This answer is the general statement about the paragraph.

25. (C)

A, B, and D happened after he started CPR.

C *Sequence* (signal: *before*) This is the only one of the answer choices that Mr. Ramirez did before he started CPR.

26. (C)

A, B, and D are facts. They can be proved.

C *Fact and opinion* This is an opinion, what someone thinks is true. Being lucky can't be proved.

27. (B)

A, C, and D Incorrect. Read paragraph 2 in the news article and "A is for Airway" in the information box. Mr. Ramirez did these steps.

B *Contrast* (signal: *all/except*) Read paragraph 2 in the news article and "A is for Airway" in the information box. This is the only thing Mr. Ramirez did not do.

28. (B)

A, C, and D are false. The informational box doesn't do any of these things.

B *Purpose* (signal: *intended to*) This is what the informational box does.

29. (A)

A *Summary* This answer summarizes the main idea of the box.

B and D are true. But they are details, not a general summary.

C This is a paraphrase of "A is for Airway." It restates the section in another way.

30. (C)

A, B, and D give sequence by age, time, and alphabet, but the animals do not sit in these orders.

C *Sequence/inference* (signal: *in order*) This is the correct sequence of the animals, beginning with Lion, the largest, and ending with Mouse, the smallest.

31. (C)

A and B No information in the reading.

C *Detail* Grizzly Bear says that Lion roars and scares away his prey.

D Incorrect. Lion does speak first.

32. (A)

A *Inference* Reread paragraph 3.

B and C No information in the reading.

D False. There are several animals between Bear and Mole.

33. (C)

A Incorrect. This is not a hint of future events in the legend.

B Incorrect. This is not a comparison, so it isn't a metaphor.

C *Figure of speech* This is one example of the figurative language that shows human feelings and actions in animals.

D Incorrect. This is not a comparison using *like* or *as*, so it isn't a simile.

34. (B)

A Incorrect. A flashback shows action from the past.

B *Imagery/detail* You can use your sense of sight to see this image.

C and D Incorrect. This passage does not express the author's purpose or theme.

35. (B)

A, C, and D Incorrect. Only one animal says
  each of these opinions.

B *Compare/Detail* (signal: *most agree*)
  In paragraph 5, Mouse says, "Nobody
  wants to burrow in the damp earth," and
  other animals murmur, "True enough."

36. (B)

A Incorrect. The word confused here is
  wheel*barrow*, which is a kind of cart.

B *Words often confused/context*
  In this sentence, *burrow* means to dig.

C The word confused here is *borrow,* which
  means to ask for money.

D Incorrect. You can get the meaning of
  thicket from paragraph 4.

37. (C)

A False. Coyote says that he wants his
  creation to look better than he does.

B False. Grizzly Bear laughs at other animals,
  too.

C *Contrast* (signal: *different from*)
  Reread paragraph 6.

D False. Coyote stays up by himself.

38. (D)

A Incorrect. A flashback shows action from
  the past.

B Incorrect. This is not a comparison, so it
  isn't a metaphor.

C Incorrect. No inference is made.

D *Opinion* In this legend, the animals give no
  facts, only opinions

39. (A)

A *Character* Coyote makes this statement
  about himself.

B No information is in the legend about
  Grizzly Bear's opinions of tails.

C and D are false. No one picks Coyote.

40. (B)

A These are not antonyms.

B *Antonyms/context* Find these words in
  paragraphs 4 and 6. They have opposite
  meanings.

C Alike. Hair and fur are similar.

D Alike. These are synonyms.

41. (A)

A *Theme* This is the general idea of the
  legend.

B False. Nothing in the legend shows
  cooperation among animals.

C and D are true, but they describe details.

42. (A)

A *Cause and effect (*signal: *because*)
  The signal *because* asks for the *cause*. This
  is in paragraph 2.

B and D These are effects, not the cause.

C No information in the reading.

43. (B)

A, C, and D don't fit the context.

B *Context* Katrin makes tiles, so an artisan
  must be skilled.

44. (C)

A and B are false. There is no mention of
  bricks or masonry in the reading.

C *Inference* Meyer says that he is a
  stonemason who makes boulders into
  blocks "for the castle's walls." You can
  infer from the context that boulders are
  large stones.

D Katrin makes tiles for the castle's floors,
  not walls.

45. (A)

A *Main idea* (signal: *mainly about*)
  This is the main idea of these paragraphs.

B This is a detail.

C and D have no information in the reading.

46. (D) *Detail* (signal; *Where*)

A, B, and C. Meyer is not from these places.

D   Reread paragraph 4.

47. (A)

A   *Summary/main idea* This states the general idea of the paragraph.

B   No information in the reading.

C   False. The reading says that the pace of life is slow. It does not mean they work slowly.

D   This is about a detail.

48. (C)

A   These were jobs of two people in the story, but the jobs are not alike.

B   A boulder is stone and planks are wood.

C   *Synonyms* Reread paragraph 1. These are two terms for the same time in history.

D   These are different actions.

49. (A)

A   *Analogy* Possible bridge sentence: *You carve wooden handles and you sew silk dresses*. This analogy shows an action and the finished product made by that action.

B, C, and D do not fit the bridge sentence.

50. (D)

A, B, and C are definitions of *last* that don't fit the context.

D   *Multiple-meaning word* Find *last* in paragraph 9: *last a thousand years*. Put each of the four definitions of *last* in the sentence. Only *survive* makes sense.

51. (D)

A   The people are using techniques from 800 years ago.

B   The same tools are used as were in the Middle Ages.

C   The passage does not talk about what happened in the past.

D   *Setting* (signal: *When*) The work is taking place now.